# Entrepreneurship, Polycentrism, and Elites

## Local Industrial Development in Modern Italy

Carlo Carboni

Francesco Orazi

AAKAR

Entrepreneurship, Polycentrism, and Elites: Local Industrial Development in Modern Italy
*Carlo Carboni and Francesco Orazi*



First Published 2019

ISBN 978-93-5002-598-7



*Published by*
**AAKAR BOOKS**
28 E Pocket IV, Mayur Vihar Phase I
Delhi 110 091 India
aakarbooks@gmail.com

*Laser Typeset at*
Sakshi Computers, Delhi

Printed at
D.K. Fine Art Press, Delhi

# Contents

# Foreword

I have known and debated with the authors of this book while they were writing it. Carlo Carboni as a visiting Professor at the Institute of Social Sciences in Delhi, Francesco Orazi in my study and teaching stay in Italy. With both I immediately shared the basic interpretation: economic development can be analysed and understood only in relation to cultural and political factors.

Un modello di sviluppo è sempre influenzato dal suo contesto sociale e questa influenza è decisiva per comprenderne caratteristiche e strutture. Inoltre, sono rimasto persuaso dal parallelismo tra certe caratteristiche italiane e indiane che gli autori mi hanno suggerito sin dai primissimi scambi di ricerca avuti con loro. Infatti, pur considerando le importanti differenze strutturali, demografiche e culturali fra India e Italia, entrambe appaiono caratterizzate da un peculiare policentrismo politico-istituzionale e da una certa importanza dei localismi nelle vie intraprese per attivare lo sviluppo economico (sviluppo locale). Questa ipotesi, pur se tenuta sottotraccia nel libro ne rappresenta una cifra interpretativa importante e ardita. In definitiva, sia il radicamento sociale, culturale e politico dello sviluppo che da Weber alla Nuova Sociologia Economica ha caratterizzato la riflessione disciplinare, sia i possibili tratti di similitudine tra India e Italia rappresentano lo fondo entro cui a mio giudizio va letto *Entrepreneurship, Polycentrism, and Elites: Local Industrial Development in Modern Italy*.

This book is the outcome of the committed social science research of these two experts in the field. It is indeed a special contribution in this much coveted area of social and economic development, and a must read for all concerned about local development and industrialization.

The focal areas the authors have undertaken for field study are "three strategic aspects which may provide guidance for the future" not only for Italy but other countries as well.

The first strategic aspect is the Italian model of local development, a crossroads in the globalization of markets which imposes an either/or choice: decline or change? The Italy of the industrial districts constitutes an innovative experience of growth in the country's manufacturing structure and entrepreneurial density. At the same time, this development was activated upon a centuries-old layering of economic, cultural, social, institutional and technological backwardness.

The second, more theoretical aspect concerns the possibility of rebuilding the institutional foundations of local development by freeing it from a rigid course of path dependence. From this viewpoint, the furrow of history, like a railway line, guides the course taken by institutions in the *longue durée*, which always remains the same.

And, the third aspect concerns the role of politics in the activation, sustaining and consolidation of the economy, as well as the risk of failure in its institutions.

The research outcome of this study is highly relevant for developing countries, especially India. India with 1.3 billion population and a strong democratic ethos has been building the local government system over the years, particularly in the rural areas where the country's 70 per cent of the population live. How is it making an impact on industrialization and social development in Indian society is an extremely important issue. I sincerely hope that this will be a critical theme for academic research as well as intellectual discourse in the days to come.

New Delhi
April 11, 2019

**George Mathew**
Chairman
Institute of Social Sciences

# Introduction

In the second half of the twentieth century, Italy has become one of the most industrialized countries in the world: in Europe, it is still the second most industrialized country, behind Germany. There are those who believe it is a disadvantage because in the more developed countries service activities are much stronger than industrial ones (United States and Great Britain). However, after the economic crisis, it was highlighted that, as far as employment is concerned, the manufacturing industry still offers holding margins and growth despite its increasing robotic automation.

Italy has become an industrial country for the economic boom of its north-west, driven in the 1950s and 60s by large companies encouraged by state investments and "reconstruction" after the Second World War. However, Italy has become the second industrialized European country thanks to the widespread industrialization of small local medium-sized enterprises in rural contexts, where a rural urban continuum was established for a phase around small and medium-sized municipalities. It is located mainly in the centre and east of the Italian peninsula (Terza Italia) and was the best local development for the country since the Renaissance, which saw its epicentre in these areas.

Local development may deal with other activities such as tourism, as in the case of the "pleasure district" formed with the epicentre of Rimini (centre-north-east) or even in a protected park area as in the case of the small villages of the Abruzzo

National Park. The book, however, focuses on the model of local industrial development of the Third Italy (centre-north-east Italy). The model of success in the 1970s and 80s is discussed by highlighting its deep roots in society, in its history and in its laborious and resilient social culture. It is a social construction in John Searle terms.

However, we also reflect on the issues that have arisen with the entry into the new century, which has shown that the miracle of its development (strong increase in GDP per capita, employment, development without too many social tears, but with low technology) was a limitation unavoidable in a global world with technological drive. In short, the quality of the niche product is not enough, but it is necessary for today's Italy that SMEs become 4.0 systems. Like big companies—big buyers of technologies—even the industrial systems of small and medium-sized companies—that we call industrial districts—must follow the high path of digitization. It is the way to reiterate that one can become great while remaining small, weaving relationships with global value chains. It is the only way to support a productivity that can distribute a moderate growth dividend in favour of maintaining employment. Something very similar is happening in Japan and Germany, which like Italy, a lower step, is expected with a decrease in the active labour force by 2030.

Obviously in Asia and, especially in the Indian subcontinent, the development paths appear to be late, but impressive and, in some respects, antithetical compared to the developed West. For example, in India according to the latest report of the McKinsey Global Institute by 2030 the workforce will increase by 138 million units, which will have to find employment. It is evident that in this case, technological productivity assumes a different social meaning and its rate at a widespread level will be on average low, but with sustained economic growth. (In September 2018, 2 billion mobile phones were exceeded in India, but this is an index of consumption and not of an endogenous technological development).

If the technological node is the current problem of a country traditionally manufacturing for its small industries spread in about 800 industrial districts, the model that has brought to the fore the local industrial development of the Third Italy in the 1980s (the studies of Piore, Sabel, Storper, etc.) may be of interest to those lagging countries such as Eastern European countries or some areas of India itself. Small businesses, small cities, widespread anthropization in the territory, strong cultural traditions.

Of course India is not Italy. Rather it can be compared to Europe, with its 29 states and 7 territories, with 24 different languages and 2,000 dialects. Indian territories are very different in terms of development and industrialization, but many of them are comparable with the characteristics belonging to the local Italian development that we describe here: small capitals, proto-industrial sectorial specialization, a social culture with a strong propensity to self-employment. These are factors that experience three stages of local development: (i) spontaneous, (ii) institutionalized and (iii) technological change. A development path through these stages requires a knowledge of the internal market, of having partnerships with other similar global areas, binding to global value chains.

The first chapter is a historical-social reconstruction (i) of the take-off of the social economic growth of the Third Italy model, (ii) of the institutional recognition, and (iii) of its crisis that requires a more technological industrial production and technological products. In the spontaneous take-off phase we show that the Third Italy already contained some important ingredients for its economic development. In the second stage of development, local institutions also become protagonists of local growth that requires institutional recognition—the industrial district—and economic, social and political local governance.

The second chapter presents a theoretical review of the sociological and economic literature on the model of Italian development, as well as highlighting a fair presence of literature in English on the subject. This analysis focuses on the flexible specialization of this Italian economic pattern which is very different from the rigidity of Fordist solutions. The theoretical review is accompanied by a detailed analysis of the profound change during the last 30 years of local societies, which are increasingly integrated with the cultural, consumer and technological expressions of society, national, European and global.

The third chapter concerns the local institutions that give life to the Italian geographical polycentrism. Territorial social differences boosted a policy of regional federalism of the Italian state. Today this federalism appears to be decommissioned by the nationalist sovereignty that the same Northern League has embraced. This party used to consider its internal enemy the Italian centralist state and its capital Rome, called the thieving city. However, today we think that the "external" enemy is the federalism between European states: and Brussels has become the thieving city. The chapter deals with topics such as the local ruling classes, the public debts of the various local administrations, their different cultural and administrative structures that can be traced back to the eight states that existed in Italy earlier, more than a century and a half ago.

The book is a cross-section of the overall Italian development. Italy can be considered a microcosm that contains all the imbalances and territorial differences that can be observed in the European macro-areas. Its north can now be considered integrated with the more developed European continental shelf. The centre represents a local development in transition to a more visible technological change. The late south risks accumulating more socio-economic backwardness.

For these reasons, we believe this volume is useful, with just a few pages presenting one of the most interesting cases of local industrial development, outside the mainstream of the industrial economy which saw in Fordism and Taylorism the best way for industrialization. Here, on the contrary, it is argued that big fish cannot always consume the smallest one that flickers faster and its flexibility, that has social roots, can be an advantage in global markets. Technology appears to be the key to the future.

The authors thank the readers and commentators of this comprehensive study, in particular Dr. George Mathew, Chairman of the Institute of Social Science in Delhi—where a large part of the book was written—and Jehanara Wasi who has edited the book. They also thank the Rector, Professor Sauro Longhi, and the Vice-Rector Gianluca Gregori who have supported this publication in many ways including the sabbatical year granted to Professor Carboni in 2018.

Delhi, December 2018

---

Carlo Carboni is the author of Chapter 1 and paragraphs 3.1, 3.2, 3.3, 3.4, 3.5, Franscesco Orazi wrote Chapter 2 and paragraphs 3.6, 3.7, 3.8.

## Map of Industrial Districts in Italy (ISTAT)

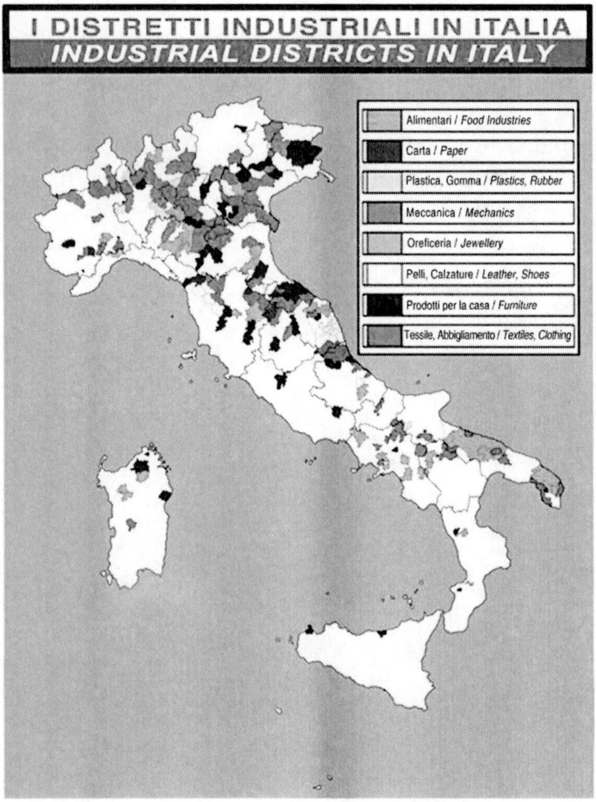


| Region | N. RO | % |
|---|---|---|
| LOMBARDIA | 42 | 24% |
| MARCHE | 34 | 19% |
| VENETO | 29 | 16% |
| EMILIA ROMAGNA | 24 | 14% |
| TOSCANA | 19 | 11% |
| PIEMONTE | 15 | 9% |
| UMBRIA | 5 | 3% |
| FRIULIV GIULIA | 3 | 2% |
| LAZIO | 2 | 1% |
| TRENTINO A A | 2 | 1% |
| LIGURIA | 1 | 1% |
| Total Center-North | 176 | 100% |

# 1

# Rise and Changes of Italian Local Development

## 1.1 Three Stages of Local Development in Third Italy

On several occasions, observers and scholars have pointed out the pivotal role played in the last 30-40 years by the local Italian economy development. It is an endogenous development, a self-generating one, combining ingredients as local factors of economic, socio-cultural and historical character.[1]

Within the economic and sociological literature it has consolidated the idea that the industrialization of our country took place not so much thanks to the great *Fordist* industry in the north-west, as the spread of small and medium industrial enterprises in local and semi-peripheral territorial contexts, some of which were defined by Becattini as *industrial districts*, i.e. local communities of companies and people.[2] With this expression, the Italian economist emphasizes two elements: (i) the importance of technical cooperation between firms that occurs in a district-sector (for example, textiles, footwear, etc.), (ii) the relevance of socio-context roots of the enterprises, mostly small and medium-sized (SME). The "local", understood in the socio-cultural and institutional context, can contribute decisively to create value and economic development. Therefore, the local economy is deeply rooted in the social, local community. Community social cohesion has represented in the past, an essential vector for take-off development. Even today, the social capital[3] is considered an economic factor of production at the economic level.

The international social literature has long since occupied the local development stimulated by the successes—production and employment—obtained by the *Made in Italy* industrial districts[4] (as well as tourism and, in part, green economy). Therein, in the 1980s it has become a growing conviction that local development denoted not only an alternative to the *Fordist* industrial economic growth, but also a path of social development "non-traumatic", unlike the one best configured by the *Fordist* development ("one company, one town").

Local development is thus a significant issue for some academic disciplines, including economic sociology, and especially for those who work at the local level in the field of industrial, economic and social policies.

The theories of local development show on the one hand, that every territory follows its own particular path. On the other hand, they point out that some regional areas (Veneto, Marche, Tuscany, etc.), which are more fully characterized by local development systems, are similar to the special synergies that occur between economic factors and social factors (cultural and institutional). They give rise to "diffuse" territorial, with high density of entrepreneurs. These regions constitute a homogeneous macro-regional area which Bagnasco refers to as *Third Italy* and what Fuà calls NEC (North-East-Centre Italy), a distinct social formation from north-west as well as from southern Italy (*Mezzogiorno*).[5]

At the diachronic level, by contrast, the issue of the different stages of development which were experienced by localism over the last forty-fifty years has been inadequately discussed. Though we have now perceived the profound transformation and the phase of changing local development. To understand this transformation, it may be useful to distinguish at least three stages of local development in the aforementioned regional areas:

- *A spontaneous (maverick) stage*: The take-off of industrial development, from the 1960s to the 70s, of which we will give a brief account given the large existing social literature on the emergence of SMEs in urban and rural areas of diffused economy.[6]
- *The maturity stage*, during the 1980s and 90s, when the emergence of *small is beautiful*, culminating in a high given institutional attention to industrial clusters.
- *The relative decline/innovation stage*, since the last years of the twentieth century till today, during which there is a noticeable fogging of Italian local development, as a consequence of the rise of the so-called turbo-capitalism, which is promoted by financial, technological, globalist forces. In this third phase, compounded by the recent economic slowdown, the "local" seems to have become opaque with the advent of globalization, like the small and medium enterprises crushed between the economies of scale achieved by large corporations foot loose (on the loose) and competitive advantages of new aggressive competitors, especially from large emerging countries such as China, India and Brazil.

Before analysing these phases, it will be appropriate to define what is meant by a localism. For now, we must keep in mind the statistical definition that formalizes it as a Local System of Labour (henceforth SLL), that is, an inter-communal territory with a high degree of population self-containment (over 70 per cent). This implies a large part of the inhabitants of the SLL working in the same territory in which it resides. Localism then means that residence and work are seen in tandem as a territorial social community.

## 1.2 The Stage of Spontaneous Local Development

The spontaneous stage is characterized by endogenous and self-generating local development, which essentially leverages on local economic and human resources. Not surprisingly, Massimo Paci, one of the most acclaimed scholars of this stage of development, emphasized that some semi-peripheral economies (especially the Marche region, the subject of his studies) were developing locally, "on their own", both far from the Fordist path which adds big cities to large industries, and far from centralized state policies, mainly aimed at bridging the gap between the north and the south.[7] According to Paci, this semi-peripheral economic development, occurred with the spread in the area of micro and small enterprises, particularly in traditional sectors (fashion, furniture, partly mechanical) creating a common economic backdrop in the territory, not centralized by the large urban web.[8] Work ethics and culture of self-employment, as we shall see, were the main springs through which the self-generating development acquired functionality and compactness.

Moreover, the scenario of the 1950s and 60s in Italy was dominated by industrialization and the birth of a Fordist society, at least in the big cities of the north-west, where the increasing urbanization produced new rhythms and new social organization, a new meeting between big business and the state. On the contrary, local development occurs in semi-peripheral regions which are characterized by rural-urban *continuum*, as well as by the relative impact of the two main regulation forces of the national power (i.e. the state and the large market forces).

However, researchers were quick to point out that the relative absence of state policies in terms of (social and education policies) constituted a social context limit for local development. For example, the stage of spontaneous development was not only accompanied by the most disparate forms of illegal work and precarious jobs, but also by a strong school dropout by adolescents and young people, who preferred to work rather than attend school (driven both by traditional work ethic and, then, by consumer expectations).

The relative lack of centralist state policies in semi-peripheral NEC economies would have produced perverse effects if some local social nets and also a certain dynamism of local institutions would not have worked: in short, the family and community cohesion of the municipalities. But we have to take into account that in 1961, a century after the unification of Italy, almost half of the Venetian homes had no running water (48 per cent), three out of four without bathrooms (72 per cent), one out of six without electricity (15 per cent): a situation slightly better than that of some regions of the *Mezzogiorno* (Southern Italy plus Island).

Within the north-west, the sudden Fordist industrialization (during the 1950s and 1960s) had issued an unprecedented economic boom, but also led to serious social problems, due to migration of our southern people to the north. Within the Fordist model rooted in the so-called *industrial triangle* (Milan-Turin-Genoa), the process of industrialization took advantage of immigrant labour from southern Italy. Fordism plus Taylorism work organization could finally use unskilled labour: the common worker without any education or qualifications, often even below age.

Besides the attraction exerted by the big companies that was synonymous with progress, the emigration to northern Italy was accelerated by the mass media such as radio, telephone and, in 1954, by television. In 1958 the municipalities of Turin, Genoa and Milan roughly "recorded 69,000 new residents—historian Paul Ginsborg writes– in 1962 this number rose to 203,800 new units." It is obvious that to urbanize this mass of southerns has been very difficult.[9]

The cities of the industrial triangle changed face. And also the surrounding countryside changed. The southern social web, after emigration, became more anaemic for the young workforce. Where the Fordist model was better developed, it had resulted in a perfect combination between the large factory and the city, according to the model "one-company, one town". A coincidence of interests is sometimes so narrow as to make the destiny of a wide urban area dependent on strategies of a large company. It is a relationship so close as to invest, beyond the economic-productive sphere, even the socio-political and cultural ones. Migration flows had led to a population growth of large cities. In Milan, near the unhealthy *coree* of a suburb that was spreading visibly, growing like mushrooms the concrete block of public housing, but also the first skyscraper, the famous "Pirelli". However, around the mid-60s, taking into account a hundred homes in Milan, one in seven still lacked drinking water, two out of five bathrooms and more than half central heating.[10]

The southern immigrants had to endure exploitation in the factory and overcome the persistence of hardship and social discrimination. The increasing urbanization therefore involved a new social organization but has struggled greatly to be realized. The workers' struggles at the turn of the 1960s and 70s, urged a welfare state's response to heal fractures and social conflicts fuelled by industrialization. All this created the conditions for a new model of social development, Fordist-Keynesian, a conductor of mass education, as the supply of social services on a large scale. The Fordist industrialization therefore implied a double social divide: in the north, the social distress of the common workers emigrated from the south with their families; in the south, the social hardship for the significant deprivation of the young motivated workforce: this emigration was a net loss of human resources for the south.

Since the mid-1960s, the NEC was instead engaged in an economic and industrial take-off to which it was not accompanied with a sudden social organizational change such as had occurred in the Fordist case. The persistence of a sort of rural-urban *continuum* keeps working within NEC. Indeed, a factor that characterizes the particular typical social structure of a community-based widespread industrialization scenario is a human settlement distributed in small and medium-sized cities, with no strong urban concentration phenomena, though not comparable to those induced by the Fordist development (Turin, Milan) or by the intensive growth of state headquarters (Roma).

Within Third Italy, industrialization took the foot without the appearance of serious social fractures. The change occurred in a scenario of a continuation of traditional values and institutions, while the territorial infrastructure (electricity, running water, paved roads, etc.) began to take shape. The modernization was imminent and knocking at the door.

Massimo Paci was among the first to observe empirically, in the early 1970s, a process of diffusive industrialization in semi-peripheral areas (compared to the industrial triangle and to the development of the state apparatuses in Rome as well as in southern big cities). He assumed initially that diffusive industrialization had socio-economic problems even more severe than those experienced by the common worker in large companies in the north-west. The worst treatment was evident in terms of protections and wages for the engaged workforce in small industrial and handicraft enterprises within a semi-peripheral economy such as Marche. Paci, however, argued that low wages and precarious jobs or off the books work, were socially accepted and softened within families as a regulation institution of the local labour market. Especially for the presence of an extended family pattern within which the peasant ethic urged young people and adults, male and female to work, backed by elders and relatives who had mostly managing reproductive functions, self-production and self-consumption. In the extended family a plurality of entries occurred and were acquitted by reproductive, self-production and self-consumption functions. These functions balanced out both low wages and irregular work treatments (including domestic work, especially of women)[11] and the shortage of state social services.

Not surprisingly, the industrialization for small medium enterprises did not cause a working class conflict comparable to the union of large enterprises of the north-west during the 1960s and 70s. In the Fordist industrial triangle, as seen, the heavy migration created problems such as wages, housing, social and cultural needs of the southern immigrant population marked by cultural delays and *dis-embedding*. On the contrary, within the diffusive economy of SMEs, industrialization has relied on the resident population, thereby resulting in a high rate of self-containment of the resident population. Industrialization is therefore characterized by an endogenous path of development based on the local community. This, in turn, has softened and diluted the material and cultural leap required by the industrial development.

One wonders why the Third Italy (NEC) localism—intended as community self-containment basins of the population—have managed to field one self-generating development of industrialization, as opposed to the southern localism. High density of local systems was found as much in some areas of the Third Italy and in some southern areas. Not only are regions like Veneto and Marche rich in local systems, but also regions such as Southern Calabria. While developing the industrial triangle industry attracted only partially immigration from certain regions of the NEC (thanks to "resistance" by organization sharecropping of their agriculture), in *Mezzogiorno*. The agricultural crisis pushed the landowner organization to release the excess of generic labour, more willing to emigrate for work to northern Italy.[12]

However, there are many other reasons as to why local development has spread in the Third Italy and only marginally in the south.

The first is that the regions of central and north-east Italy are contiguous to the north-west and this has encouraged herd behaviour. Geographical proximity has undoubtedly counted as a propellant for local development in the NEC, even for a certain decentralization of production flow to craft micro-enterprises. Geographical proximity has made it especially effective considering what the north-west was showing, that industrialization enabled the population access to new consumer goods, industrial goods (cars, household appliances, etc.). There was therefore an opportunity to open up to a much larger domestic market with respect to the weekly village and local markets. What was happening in the north-west had a demo effect among the inhabitants of the neighbouring regions, able to push their social expectations towards new consumption and progress of the new industrial modernity.

Endogenous economic development depends also on the rise of social expectations to new consumption not feasible with the self-production and self-consumption, typical of a traditional society. In short, the industry does not enter the door of the production to "warm hearts and expectations of the people", but from that of consumption that, in turn, creates dependence on new industrial activities (profits and wages). One does not just wish for things, but one must earn them, by producing them. So one must have means, labour force and entrepreneurship.

Even the topography has relied heavily on the spontaneous stage of local development of the Third Italy. The local endogenous and spontaneous development has developed mainly in valley sites. The latter in Italy are numerous and there are well-organized communities, the powerful industrial localism locations. They exist not only in the valleys of the Third Italy, but also in the foothills of Piedmont and Lombardy.

These casings of hilly and valleys *anthropization* often have a history that takes us back to proto-industrial presences which explain the birth of the industrial districts.[13]

In contact with the new consumption of industrial society and exposed increasingly to its message, these local casings—delimited administratively as municipalities—have gradually opened to the affluent modernity and to the scenario of new media.

How did entrepreneurship contribute to the NEC localism?

Historians have pointed out that the sharecropping and small rural properties have contributed immensely to forge an entrepreneurial spirit, as trade which was fairly well developed in the municipalities of the Third Italy, brightly ancient antecedents. In the municipal villages trade, crafts and proto-industrial production were traditionally developed: this is the cradle in which grows a microenterprise production and market. Going back to the farmer and sharecropper, they knew how calculating and possessed a farmhouse was. Sometimes, the lower floor, usually dedicated to the stables, was later used as a workshop.

Sharecropping was not only a form of agricultural economic management, but represented a way of social organization within a traditional and local realm governed by family and community. It therefore conducted a system of values and attitudes such as familism, localism, a strong work ethic and vocation to self-employment. All these were important factors, which, in turn, fuelled and encouraged confident relationships in the community. This trust was the main permissive condition for the emergence of entrepreneurship.[14] In fact, in trusting social contexts, it is more likely that individuals accept the inherent entrepreneurship risks. If the context is known and people know for closeness, for parent-family relationships, friendships, community, the propensity to risk "of their own" is encouraged by the atmosphere of the context of social protection. Entrepreneurs and workers know each other well in a local area.

All these permissive conditions occurred in the Marche as in Tuscany, but not in Calabria, where, on the contrary, this knowledge was often based on distrust because, as Banfield, observes the plot of the local relationships was undermined by amoral familism, rather than propelled by the communitarian ethic.[15] The transformation of the southern mafias into modern criminal organizations did the rest.

Moreover, taking into account historical permissive factors, unlike the southern localism, NEC regions took advantage of the prestigious history of their municipalities which, by the Renaissance flourishing times had inherited theatres, hospitals, universities and secular service facilities, even in small municipalities.[16]

Finally it should be considered that the spontaneous stage of industrial local development has made the social structure of the NEC regions quite different from the rest of Italy since the presence of a crowd of micro-entrepreneurs who, for a long period, accounted for at least one-third of total employment. The self-employment propensity is part of work ethics that has experienced a special continuity between the municipal-rural world and the industrial district one, particularly, in the regions of central Italy. The ethics of self-employment is a very special lubricant for the engine of self-generating development. This culture of work and enterprise was boosted and encouraged not only by entrepreneurship inherent in rural sharecropping, but also by businesses craftsmen that have long formed the core of the small municipalities of the NEC. In the south, on the contrary, the prevalence of agriculture landowners, that is a concentrated power, had created patronage and dependence (the wage labourers) among the majority of the population.

After recalling the most important economic, social and historical factors to explain why the diffusive industrialization has developed in some local contexts (NEC) than in others (Mezzogiorno), you need to consider the material life of the people. And then acknowledge social and environmental costs still paid by local communities for take-off of the so-called "industrialization without fractures."[17]

In the 1970s, the education of the NEC population was still depressed on average than in other regions of the north-west. The working life of the people can be symbolically summarized by the workers who alternated the activity in the industrial firm to that in rural areas, consumption of new products of industrial modernity and self-consumption. During the spontaneous stage of local development, self-consumption and self-production remained persistent, like other traditional behaviours, familism and localism. Moreover, as in the case when the aircraft takes off, the industrialization take-off burned many resources, especially the human ones. Under-wages were widespread like various forms of clandestine work. Rather than a full-employment system, one could speak of an efficient full underemployment system.[18] There were no obvious social fractures, mainly due to family dampers (the extended family) but it should be recognized that there was an environmental impact if only because the productive sectors of SMEs were often very polluting.

Environmental impact, schooling deficit, harsh working relationships: thus local development still involved great individual and community sacrifices. The presence of two strong political subcultures,[19] the Democratic and the Communist, helped to defuse possible social or class conflicts on such issues (education, labour, environment) and to legitimize the local institutional intervention: the local community interest has therefore always prevailed over the class interest.

So far we have stressed that an economic approach cannot explain neither local development nor how, when and why enterprises are founded. After the Second World War, the diffusive industrialization was favoured by the changing international division of work, as a result of the gradual disposal of industrial activities with low added value by the most advanced industrialized nations. This was the permissive condition influenced by geopolitical strategies, as is the case today for local industrial development of some regions of China. However, there were decisive permissive factors in the local context—historical and sociological in nature—which were exploited by a positive social action that characterized the peripheral economies, mainly, in Third Italy.

## 1.3 The Stage of Maturity: Industrial Districts and Local Institutions

Not only can you envisage three stages of "widespread (diffusive) economy" within the Italian local development. There are also three different waves (expansive cycles) that have expanded its range of local influences to create an original social formation, even more extensive than Third Italy.

A first wave of local development involved—since the1960s—Emilia Romagna, Tuscany and, partly, Veneto and Marche (but also the valley areas of the north-west). A second wave in the 1970s covered the Umbria, the north-east and the Marches as a whole. A third filtered down to Abruzzo and, to a limited extent, along the Adriatic in the south-eastern territories (according to G. Fuà, the Adriatic road to industrial development).[20]

Now let us ask ourselves: what are the factors that have marked the mature stage of local development?

The first factor relates to the increasing importance of the institutions. In the mature stage, the pattern of local development in diffused-based on small and medium enterprises. The economy has indeed highlighted the need for facing and managing social, infrastructural and environmental problems: hence the role of institutions and, in particular, the local ones. Local development accompanied the regionalist and municipalist decentralization. Since the 1980s, the conditions of the complex process of decentralization of functions and powers from the central state to local and regional authorities have been created.

Local institutions, in areas of local development, have forged new relationships and strengthened the territorial social capital. They have become guarantors of the local citizenship system. For example, during the 1970s and 80s, Emilia before and then Umbria and Marche showed the highest educational rating among Italian regions. Consider also that several surveys have pointed out that, in particular, in Central Italy citizens give more credibility to local institutions than other Italian contexts.[21] The quality of life (social, health and environmental protection) was indeed associated with economic growth as a complementary face, but essential for sustainable local development.

The fact that in regions of small and medium enterprises the good economic performance has been progressively associated with a high quality of life, made it more credible as a pattern of development, especially in the presence of the Fordist way of development that was now in a phase of terminal crisis. In fact, starting from the second half of the 1980s, in the regional and national areas dominated by the great Fordist enterprise, has highlighted a widening gap between economic growth and social development. The jobless growth (economic growth without additional work) was typical of this gap which emerged from the mid-1980s and early 90s. The largest industrial enterprise has lost jobs and its main social function (creation of relatively stable jobs).[22]

The prevalence of one of the two major parties—DC or PCI—in the regions of Third Italy undoubtedly favoured the community cohesion and the regional and local institutions activism. In this case Veneto, the most important party (DC) has ruled the central state, while subordinately maintaining a dialogue with the local civil society. In Emilia Romagna, the most popular party (PCI), in opposition to the central government, had a strong interest in locally consolidating the socio-economic development by solid institutional roots. In the Emilia-Romagna case, local institutions have contributed to greatly to supporting local development at the economic and social level, compared to what happened in Veneto. In fact, the Emilia Romagna has become, in the 80s, an emblematic case not only of regional economic growth through local development (one of the richest regions of Europe), but also in terms of building the local welfare services. The Veneto, instead, still laments the weak ineffective action of local institutions (infrastructure and services deficit).

Even the institutionalization of local development (the introduction of industrial district committees, policies for local development) was another sign of institutional maturity of some regions to diffusive economy. Therefore a second factor which denotes access to a mature stage of local development is the visibility of the industrial districts (IDs), a phenomenology that is halfway between the economy and society: the best known, celebrated and acclaimed form of local development.

The local industrial development, in many cases, has been consolidated in the image of the neo-Marshallian industrial district that Becattini's successful interpretation made paradigmatic.[23]

According to industrial economists, the ID is an aggregation of SMEs located in a limited area (mostly just a supra-dimension). Industrial economists who are more sensitive to the "social atmosphere of the district" stressed that, in order to appreciate the existence of the district, it is crucial to have not only the presence of a community of firms, but also one of the local citizens. The local community is an important social cement, for creating networks of enterprises. Not surprisingly, local development occurs in high social cohesion local communities. Hence the thesis that socio-contextual factors are decisive to offer competitive advantages to the economy. According to Becattini, the ID is a single-sector because the commodity uniformity is the only one able to empower the collaboration between enterprises, even in a hierarchy and a technical division of locally-based activities.

The economic and social literature on IDs in Italy is now quite extensive, even regarding the attention that these forms of territorial development have attracted internationally. The industrial districts demonstrate that you can be big even while small. Much of the 'Made in Italy' is in fact produced by the light industry of the districts, which embodies flexible forms[24] suited for export of their products.[25] Much of the local development paradigm is indebted to these local highly industrialized forms, which, as we said, have very high indices of entrepreneurial density.

The visibility of the Italian industrial districts, in large part localized in Central—North Italy—particularly in NEC—rose to their continued performance over the last 25-30 years in terms of economic and job growth,[26] but, as I said, even as the quality of social life.[27] Meanwhile, it also increased political visibility of small and medium entrepreneurs, increasingly crucial as a social group in the political and institutional developments, in particular between the 1980s and 90s. If public opinion is suddenly aware of the virtues of the districts and the politics and institutions are having to appreciate the political and social weight of small and medium entrepreneurs, the social sciences, economic, financial and organizational sociology continued to keep under examining the IDs.

So much attention in multiple dimensions has led the regional and local institutions (which have now greatly increased their powers) to adopt measures in order to support industrial districts. In fact, in the maturity stage of local development, industrial districts have not only been consolidated under the institutional form (local governing bodies), but in many cases they have diversified and have moved away from the Becattini neo-Marshallian definition.[28]

The most successful IDs appeared precisely as those who have undergone major diversification of the product, demonstrating their strong production flexibility (multi-sector districts), spurred by export vocation of these systems. Their evolution confirms the idea that districts renew an ancient tradition of expansion, crisis and restructuring that are repeated cyclically. Since the early 1990s of the last century, we have seen the cyclical crises of mono (single)-sectorial districts such as the so-called "Scarponia", straddling the Macerata and Fermo, or the Prato textile industry.

The stage of maturity coincides with the years of celebration of small is beautiful and made in Italy. However, at this time the crises of neo-Marshallian districts go unnoticed as well as the rapid transformation of many of them, both in terms of sector diversification (multi-sector districts), which in terms of size and organizational (core districts, with medium-large enterprises).[29] While celebrating the small size, some medium and large enterprises were beginning to emerge, from Benetton to Stefanel, Del Vecchio and Merloni, from Bombassei to Della Valle. Within the undergrowth of tens of thousands of SMEs also trees grew which today are medium and large industrial organizations which can have their say not only on the international market circuit, but also in political terms and policies.

In the early 1990s, the district areas show more positivity in terms of exports, sales growth and jobs, but also, contrary to the economic vulgate without empirical basis, in terms of innovation. Now it becomes clear that Italy became an industrial country thanks to SME clusters and to the locally diffused economy. However, the celebration of small enterprise and 'Made in Italy' insidiously relegates to the background the transformations, the evolutions, the diversification of the district areas and prevents a serious analysis of the early troubles of these local lungs of the Italian industry, especially in the case of mono-sector districts, labour intensive and with low value-added.

The 1980s and early 90s, therefore, constitute a period of maturity reached by the majority of regional economies based on diffusive industrialization, localism and districts. But, as we shall see, the pitfalls are around the corner.

The 80s, years of maturity, celebrate the pattern of flexible specialization of SMEs[30] as a real alternative to the Fordist one.[31] In fact, regional economies such as Marche, Tuscany and Emilia-Romagna, after subscribing to the Chinese current rates, in the 80s, recorded growths in the Italian media and in fact begin a slow reorganization of the activities that would lead, in recently years, to a network of services and trade sustaining industrial economy.

The labour market slowly settles and reduces forms of black market labour within the industry. Within the rural economy self-production and self-consumption evaporate overwhelmed by mass industrial consumption. In NEC, the activity and employment rates, even female ones, remain the highest in Italy, but the distances are reducing gradually, as some of the consequences of aging begin to take shape.

However, the strength of the pattern of industrial SMEs in the maturity phase is out of the question. Not only did the export of 'Made in Italy' increase and consolidate, but the pattern expands its radius of influence: also other areas appear infected, especially along the Adriatic road of industrialization, with Abruzzo and then, with the Puglia and southern IDs.[32]

If the presence of institutions and districts is revealing, they have reached a stage of maturity of the local industrial development. Some social transformations—for depth and size—determine new social scenarios of local development.

The rise of education is one of these elements, measured by schooling rates. It is no coincidence that in all NEC regions, the period of greatest industrial growth (but with low school enrolment rates) was followed by a phase of intense schooling (but with medium industrial growth). Most institutional presence gradually erodes behaviours and traditional practices: the school and higher university education spread, changing the traditional rules of use of the young workforce within the logic of the firm-family, now in steep decline as an agency which regulates the local labour market.

The gradual overcoming of colloquial or slang terms and the progressive affirmation of communication national language, are associated with the spread of consumerist behaviour in part contrary to traditional logic "save and gain", to enter the trap of " I work, so I spend." The traditional family is now not only in front of the workings of large social cross-levelling such as education, health and social services, communication, consumption of products (not just local) but also at the centre of a major reversal of the demographic trend, with record rates of increase in the elderly population. The traditional, extended family gives way to drier families, modern in using time: the "family inn" appears as the heir of the traditional extended family, a family in which the traditional hierarchical relationships, based on the couple *authority/obedience*, are gradually replaced, as advocated by Alessandro Cavalli, as the contractual modern-oriented couple *exchange/agreement*.

Changing consumption and the social horizon expands within which the national social imagination is now travelling. The improvement of infrastructure and communication networks gradually erodes the importance of local short bonds in favour of the national and international ones. Consider, for example, the role of exports, tourism, communication media and culture.

The family conforms to the individual empowerment process, but it is now downgraded in its socio-economic and educational functions. Local areas open increasingly to the double sense of belonging (to the local and national, to the dialect and Italian). It is therefore impossible to think about the maturity of the local development pattern by omitting institutional and social changes to which we have referred. The drives of thought and mentality are gradually replaced by other references more related to modernity.

This local development pattern still offers a climate of trust and business and civic engagement, but the mechanisms have now to be adapted to the new national scenario. We could argue that the local social capital is now increased not only through relationships and tacit know-how, but also by the new social and cultural assets (primarily education) and by the eruption of national modernity in social relations. A true social change. The growing importance of national and international dimension will downsize the local development pattern embedded in the traditional contexts. There is a transformation/ erosion of local culture, although the continuity of civicness remains.

For firms in the districts, the importance of tacit knowledge is now relative, while more and more relevant encoded knowledge develops, new professional knowledge in times of technological change. Gradually the social context loses importance, with its traditional local and family networks. What emerges is the importance to manage local development management, especially in IDs. You start talking about district governance, as a conscious strategy in order to boost the cooperation between enterprises by involving their social context activism. The district governance pursues objectives of development and improvement of the territory. This new awareness of local development actors however meets political elites which are unprepared for industrial policies for SMEs and for their local contexts. We are now in the 1990s, and in Italy, one of the biggest problems is to implement governance policies supporting innovation and internationalization of our industrial localism. Moreover, the lack of industrial policy which Italy nowadays records, appeared clear from the years just celebrating the maturity of local development.

## 1.4 Decline or Breakthrough?

As mentioned, local development is understood as a complex phenomenon which refers to economic, social, historical, institutional factors, so onto the pitch of interdisciplinary analysis on communication networks and professionalism, on local cultures and social capital, on orographic and historical features. In particular, economic sociology has forced the concept of local development in favour of a neo-institutional approach,[33] proposing governance solutions, both (i) the institutional form of "negotiated planning" promoted by the central state to locally support socio-economic actors (ii) boost some large IDs institutionally defined and recognized at the regional level.

The concept of local development is more general than that of the industrial district. Local development is a phenomenology not reducible to economic interpretation only. It can be realized not only with industrialization, but also, for example, with tourism or the enhancement of the environmental and cultural activities. Since the second five years of the 1990s, in the global world local development is no longer identifiable with the Italian and German industrial districts, but with new much wider regional localism of the BRIC (Brazil, Russia, India and China) or localism manufacturers to new technologies and services (the example of Silicon Valley and Hyderabad-Bangalore). In addition, to the presence of globalization, the introduction of the hybrid term glocal has not solved some of the ongoing problems of territorial rescaling. Rather the question is whether it still makes any sense to emphasize the local development pattern in a globalized world.

We can say that local development in the global scenario no longer means Italian classic ID, but refers to wider regional territories in developing countries or developed countries that have found a place in the new international division of production determined by the global, technological and financial changes that have characterized the fifteen years before the last large economic-financial crisis.

Since the 1990s of the last century, as it has consolidated the great technological change and has established a new economy,[34] local development and the Italian industrial districts are back to being phenomena that affect at risk of downgrading territories, as producing traditional products for which there is now an abundant supply in the international markets due to fierce competition that countries in the developing world are able to carry, making use of a smaller cost factor.

The paradigm of the horizontal network, now dominant in the social and economic culture, has led some scholars to reconsider the explanatory power of industrial districts, including their governance. This position has passed with the ID concept within a network global economy: enterprise networks, network companies, industrial networks even in distant lands, market networks, financial networks, technology networks, infrastructure networks, communication and information networks. The global network available to end up overwhelmed the visibility of the districts.

The global focus is now on a long network of large corporations which traditionally are big buyers of computer science and automation and key players in the economic and cultural globalism (the prevalence of corporate cultures). Moreover, the concept of network-enterprise also precedes the boom of the network of networks, that is Internet. The ID, which although had contributed to suggesting the concept of network (district as an enterprises network) again becomes a second hand localism, the limits of which are evident in times of intensive technological innovation and strong competition. The Italian IDs appear as part of localism, showing a deficit of advanced knowledge and communication services (the fever of the new economy) must frantically use their traditional methods to compete and gain global visibility. The large organizational hierarchies foot loose, transnational economic archipelagos spring the focus upon the benefits enjoyed by the corporate cultures in terms of deployment capabilities and for "the large volume of fire" which it can employ. The big fish comes back to consume the small fish.

In short, we are facing "difficult times" for the industrial districts and Italian local development. For some scholars, the regions become territorial platforms on which land great capitals of multinational foot loose enterprises attracted by environmental conditions favourable to produce.[35] Even Italian IDs enterprises are the first to betray their roots, moving their production firms abroad where the cost of factors of production are more profitable than in the mother country, especially for what concerns the labour cost. In other words, the district is losing within the global networks that its own enterprises help to weave.

During the 90s the number of local areas infected by the new localization of multinationals is also increasing. Think of Europe in the case of Ireland or the Basque Country, but especially in Asia, China and India, in the meantime develop in the 90s with a growth rate close to 9 per cent per year. The competition between territories to attract foreign investment (FDI) is perhaps more important than that between products. This partly changes the meaning of local development, now dependent on the international framework.

Moreover, research makes clear that our small enterprises are struggling not so much in the innovation process, but to innovate products and methods of transaction.[36] For example, we see how electronic communication informs the nervous system of our industrial enterprises, that is what the new economy is widespread in terms of e-business. The percentage of users of IBS rises to 50 per cent of our enterprises, when considering those with more than 250 employees. This is "the proof" of the fragility of our productive structure in the face of new technologies and the world of research and innovation. So, at best, it is a noticeable backwardness, at worst, the sign of a decline in progress. Several scholars—given the weakness of our large enterprise and the fragility of our districts—argue that the decline is much more than a threat to our country.[37]

What is happening in recent years should however be interpreted in a different and closer to what is claimed, for example, by Porter,[38] who has bent the interpretation to the reasonable assumption that the institutions and local governance forms may raise the competitiveness of its own territory, especially in terms of external economies and transaction costs. The district policies need to be further strengthened, especially on infrastructures and services and by intentional external economies. The model to aspire to, in this case, would be that of some extremely organized German Landers or of some of the Italian digitized districts.

However, the IDs, rather than getting lost in global long networks, continue to represent a very dense network of short and strong bonds, fiduciary, moral, professional: a network that has its centripetal force, which retains and locates the relations and exchanges, otherwise sucked into the global dispersion. The local development continues at the bottom to exercise a high degree of self-containment of the population, assured by this centripetal force which, if organized, can communicate with the global centrifuge force. So the stronger the centripetal force the more this dense network can locally be a visible node of global networks, long networks, weak and increasingly relevant, according to the Granovetter's theory.[39]

Moreover, in recent years, new entrepreneurs have emerged from the localism international profile (like Del Vecchio, Della Valle, Bombassei to name a few) and even a fourth capitalism formed by medium-sized enterprises, mostly targeted at global niche markets, sort of "pocket multinationals". In fact, the industrial districts are changing progressively. Often they appear in the guise of post-districts, cluster of SMEs within the middle one or more medium-large enterprises, or as a multi-sector milieu or also as meta-districts locating a node of a network of small and medium-sized high-tech enterprises. Many enterprises seek to be connected with international production chains.

Our approach is based on hypothesis of the decline of the industrial district as a traditional shape and its possible evolution-transformation, indicated by a number of organizational, technological and environmental discontinuities, which make an innovative breakthrough possible.

Today we can assume the following segmentation typological "district".

A first end of districts has traditional features, the more times indicated by Becattini: districts with strong roots in the local community, together with the tacit knowledge resources and informal "know how" and its normative precepts. But this type of district—single sector, more traditional—survived sector diversification processes, usually adopts a defensive flexibility. Overall, its small companies present—in an unfavourable current economic situation—of negative performance indicators. There is therefore a first band of traditional districts (a "community of people and a population of industrial enterprises", according to Becattini's prior definition) which presents as main ingredients the local identity and the "diffuse knowledge", cooperation and the 'integration of small and medium-sized enterprises. Today it seems in fact that the keys to success of the past have become totally inadequate in the global economy which requires the creation and the interception of other cognitive and operational, strategic and organizational, financial and technological resources. A variant of this type of district is the pseudo-district, as in some cases of local development, typically in more traditional sectors: it is a cluster of enterprises where the integration is low as much as the division of labour and cooperation between the production units. In this case, it is more difficult to have an organizational and technological turnaround of these traditional enterprises with prime competitors on the international markets.

Nowadays there is a second and third type of industrial district. We call this a multi-sector post-district, because it has been through several major turnarounds and today appears diversified by sectors, with different productive specializations within it. The other type of post-district consists of what has been called "the district with stones", i.e. local industrial development driven by one (or more) medium-large company, which effectively guides the entire local territorial development. In research on Adriatic (Centre-East) districts, the first type of post-district is well exemplified by the former accordion Ancona south district which today is a major multi-sector district that ranges from microeletronics to plastic, from toys to cartoons production. The Fabriano district is instead a typical mechanical district in which they operate large and medium leading companies such as Indesit (now Whirpool) and Elica. In post-districts, the "long networks" and the cognitive and symbolic resources, delivered in real time, make sense like the technological resources used in the speeding up or acceleration of the production-distribution process. "Short" local networks remain important, but—unlike the traditional district—are less important compared to those long for where proximity is virtual and not territorial. These districts require the presence of professional communities that can capture knowledge and innovations, thus able to increase the level of learning of the entire local system, as a premise to imitation and innovation. This evolved form of post-district, smaller firms can draw from both external economies triggered by the leader enterprises and those may be activated by the local community institutions.

Finally, there are networks of high tech, localized and concentrated mostly in urban contexts, we might call meta-districts, whose ties with the territory are strongly intermediated by the presence of innovative professional communities. The presence of these or the ability to attract them or even hold them is a basic requirement for territorial competitiveness. The meta-districts (for example, in biotechnology, communication technologies and media, the production of software) have a specific need for external economies such as universities to address science and technology, research and development institutions and public goods "local" animated by new professional urban communities. This combination of factors has raised the role of milieu innovateur exercised by the cities and more urbanized tissue, typically containers of professionalism and innovative elements. Today the wealth of regions largely depends not only on the technological equipment in the production and social spheres, as the existence of professional communities able to enable that technology in a strategic sense as a source of economic value.

Undoubtedly the three types of districts are very different, in terms of absolute weight, of added value and a long list of economic indicators, organizational, etc. Even the "case of China" can be enlightening in this regard. For district companies belonging to the first traditional districts, China is basically a dangerous competitor, while for post-districts this aspect has less importance and China promises to be more frequently as a real or potential market for the allocation of their products. For the fourth type, China has a rich potential market of products and, perhaps, of cognitive resources.

The geography of local development is therefore changing, and changes its requirements.[40]

It is possible that the three types of aggregation of SMEs share a common need to place alongside intangible and infrastructure, conductive of cognitive resources: the common need of research institutions and universities which are able to create innovative professional communities (new managers and technicians, knowledge workers, etc.).[41] Such professional communities characterized themselves as a competent connective web between universities and enterprises. There is a common requirement of knowledge and research facilities, capable of enabling local development in imitative and innovative practices, thanks to the transfer of technology and adequate professional skills. But, for now, it lacks a strategic vision that can indicate a technology-innovative path out of the current state of suspension in which we find our economic local development.

## 1.5 Short Conclusion

Organizational and technological knowledge is not yet sufficiently widespread throughout the fabric of Italian SMEs. Professional communities delay to drive a "network of enterprises". Yet a few scholars have observed that new technologies would offer new opportunities to SMEs, allowing them to access network services once reserved for large-sized companies. The virtual communication does not fit the districts, to replace traditional relations and communicative behaviours based on proximity and physical presence. For this new professional communities (human and social capital) can induce changes in the economic behaviour of our small entrepreneurs. They could build a competence network. Italian elites should first of all strengthen social capital, which is excessively crushed on localism and short relationships. In Italy, before the recent crisis there was a crowd of small entrepreneurs and the industrial (family) capitalism of the NEC was a "popular" one. However, many small enterprises are working in a subcontracting mode.

New professional communities can modernize the traditional economy and facilitate the transition to the new stage of socio-economic development. In thinking about the next coming development, innovation of professionalism in the workplace must buy more body, also regarding the transfer of technology to enterprises.[42]

The issue of professional communities (and social capital available) appears as a first major entry point to pursue a "high" trajectory of "offensive flexibility" of development, taking into account that this last is not only connected to the availability of investment and an innovative enterprise culture, but also to a new and professional content of the work. In addition, the need to strengthen the new professional communities implies that education and training of new professions are important drivers of development, especially the local one. It is not by chance that our local system is an ongoing transformation of the external economies which are useful to enterprises. In the foreground there is the rise of universities, and public and private R&D centres, and good training and recruitment systems.

Among the intangible collective goods which have greatly contributed to the new economy, the availability of advanced professional community (their competence networks) is an issue to be addressed urgently in Italian labour markets. The goal of increased production in the manufacturing sector seems not only to depend on technology transfers, but especially by the spread of new skills that can enable technologies in a strategic sense for enterprises and their business. Moreover, in Italian enterprises innovation does not approve the search field of activity and development, but rather relates to the application/imitation of new technologies to the process and the product. Dissemination of the professional community is not an easy goal to achieve: the United States, as mentioned, continues to import engineers to bridge the deficit of their professional areas. Local development will be able to open fully to the new technologies if this new issue is governed within the professional labour market.

The problem is this: who will manage the breakthrough? Above all, who can do it, given the limits demonstrated by our elites[43] and local collective actors?

In this regard, Trigilia returned to the theme of local governance and the importance of the institutions in the management of this breakthrough that he called a project for Italy.[44] However, the impression is that the issue of governance has given poor fruits even when, in the 1990s, Italian local development was at its height. Perhaps, in order to handle the economic declining threats, Italians should agree to drop the idea of a country made up of a thousand localisms and, instead, consider it divided into a few macro-regions within the global scenario.

The density of IDs and enterprises makes NEC an industrial region. According to Marshal, the industrial region is the natural culmination of a development for IDs of small and medium-sized enterprises.

In short, the issue of the districts and local development seems effectively evaporated and overcome by their own evolution. It would therefore be appropriate to accept the idea of the decline of Italian traditional local municipal and provincial development characterized by SMEs. Rather, the regional industrial area of the so-called Third Italy medium and large enterprises have grown that constitute economic organizations able to compete with new economies of scale. So it has to adhere to the idea that the actors who can implement the necessary change are, besides the central and regional institutions, the robust body of medium- large enterprises that appear to have what it takes in terms of innovation and internationalization. This is the perspective of the fourth capitalism supported by several scholars.[45] Of course, you also need a banking system capable of stimulating an innovative finance, without which you do not go anywhere, as shown by the path traced by the most advanced countries, which have already envisaged governance. In addition, Italy needs, above all, an entrepreneurial culture that recreates the animal spirits of the market and that drop entrepreneurship domesticated by politics and assistance. This does not mean that we should abandon the path of sustainable development, an economy to social service. It simply means that it takes more competitive entrepreneurship (more competition and thus market) more efficient and transparent institutions for a better redistribution of wealth on the social side (more education, research, new social services). There is also a necessity of territorial rescaling by creating macro-regions and a new system regulatory for a local development that can exploit all possible synergies of a "large area". Only large and well populated areas can compete for the international gate which is why big cities are ruling the global game.

## REFERENCES


1. This chapter is a re-elaboration of an online handout (2002) for the students of sociology of local systems at the "Giorgio Fuà" Faculty of Economics and for those of Urban and Rural Sociology at the Faculty of Engineering of the Polytechnic University of the Marche. The writing, therefore has an educational profile, expanded and revisited with the addition of some issues still open in the debate among specialists of the discipline.
2. Becattini G.(2001), *The Caterpillar and the Butterfly. An Exemplary Case of Development in the Italy of the Industrial Districts*, Le Monnier and ib. (1979), *Dal settore industriale al distretto industriale: Alcune considerazioni sull'unità d'indagine dell'economia industriale*, in Rivista di economia e politica industriale, n.1.
3. Orazi F. (2009), "Il capitale sociale" in Carboni C. (ed.), *La Governace dello sviluppo locale*, Il Mulino, Bologna.
4. Fortis M. (1998), *Il Made in Italy*, Il Mulino, Bologna.
5. Third Italy includes the following regions: Vento, Trentino , Friuli V.G., Emilia-Romagna, Marche, Toscana, Umbria. See Bagnasco A. (1977), *Tre Italie. La problematica territoriale dello sviluppo italiano*, Il Mulino, Bologna. Fuà G., Zacchia C. (eds.) (1983), *Industrializzazione senza fratture*, Il Mulino. Bologna.
6. Among other authors, see Moroni M. (2007), *Alle origini dello sviluppo locale. Le radici storiche della Terza Italia*, Il Mulino, Bologna.

7. Paci M. (ed.) (1980), *Famiglia e mercato del lavoro in una economia periferica*, Franco Angeli, Milano.
8. In fact, in the Third Italy, the urban centres—the "thousand historical municipalities"—are widespread in the territory with dimensions below 300,000 inhabitants.
9. Ginsborg P. (1989), *Storia d'italia dal dopoguerra a oggi. Societa' e politica 1943-19*88, Einaudi, Torino.
10. See Alasia F., Montali D. (1975), Milano *Corea*, 1975 (ed.) who describe the processes of creating urban social marginality.
11. Paci M. (1980); G. Fuà e C. Zacchia (1983).
12. Sori E. (1979), *L'emigrazione italiana dall'unita' alla seconda guerra mondiale*, Il Mulino, Bologna.
13. Moroni M. (2008).
14. Carboni C. (1994), "La Terza Italia", in (Bevilacqua P. edited by), *Lezioni sull'Italia Repubblicana*, Donzelli, Roma.
15. Banfield E.C. (1961), *Una comunita' del mezzogiorno*, Il Mulino, Bologna.
16. Putnam R. D. (1993), *Making Democracy Work: Civic Traditions in Modern Italy,* Princeton University Press.
17. Fua G. Zacchia C. (1983).
18. Paci M. (1980) and Carboni C. (1987), "Mentalità, lavoro e classi sociali", in S. Anselmi (ed.), *Le Marche*, Einaudi, Torino.
19. Trigilia C. (1986), *Grandi partiti e piccole imprese*, Il Mulino, Bologna.
20. Carboni C. (1998), L'Abruzzo regione cerniera o modello di sviluppo per il Mezzogiorno?, in Il Mulino, XLVII, n. 1. With such an abstract modelling, three groups of regions could therefore be included. And one might think that the problems of the spontaneous phase of a region like that, for example, most of the Marche region, were the same ones crossed in "adolescence" by a region of the first group, for example from Emilia-Romagna. But all this sounds like an evolutionary evolution, largely useless, as we approach our days, when the present scenario and the international element increase their pressure, consequences and

change. The general aspect of the territory is the social context of Granovetter M. (1973), The Strength of Weak Ties, in *American Journal of Sociology*, 78, pp. 1360-1380, that is unrepeatable, not replicable on the same terms. However, an evolutionist approach has a certain analytical-descriptive validity, as well as having conceptualized an economic-social formation called Terza Italia, in spite of the fact that the widespread economy, beyond this macro-region (both in the north -west than in southern areas).

21. See Presidenza del Consiglio della Regione Marche (2003), *La Polis,* Ancona.
22. Carboni C. (2004), *L'occupazione senza crescita e lo sviluppo socialmente sostenibile*, in Il Mulino n. 1.
23. Becattini G. (1979 and 2001)
24. Piore M., Sabel C. (1984), *The Second Industrial Divide*, Basic Books, New York.
25. Storper M. (1991), *Tecnology Districts and Industrial Trade* in AAVV "Undefended Cities and Regions" Athens.
26. Carboni C. (1996), *Distretti industriali, governo locale e Mezzogiorno*, in Rivista economica del Mezzogiorno, n. 4.
27. Cavalieri A. (1999), *Toscana e toscane. Percorsi locali e identita' regionale nello sviluppo economic*, Franco Angeli, Milano.
28. See Becattini G., Bellandi M., Dei Ottati G., Sforzi F. (2001), *Il caleidoscopio dello sviluppo locale*, Rosemberg e Sellier, Torino. Burroni L. (2001), *Allontanarsi crescendo: politica e sviluppo locale in Veneto e Toscana*, Rosenberg & Sellier, Torino. Alessandrini P. (eds.) (2001), *Il sistema finanziario italiano tra globalizzazione e localismo*, Il Mulino, Bologna, 2001.Trigilia C. (2001), *Patti per lo sviluppo locale: un esperimento da valutare con cura*, in "Stato e Mercato" n. 3. Balloni V., Cucculelli M., Iacobucci D. (1999), *L'industria italiana dell'elettrodomestico nel contesto internazionale*, Giappichelli, Torino. Ramella F. (2005), *Reti sociali e performance economiche nelle imprese ICT*, in Stato e Mercato n. 3.
29. Carboni C. (1996).
30. Sabel C., Zeytlin J. (1982), *Alternative storiche alla produzione di massa*, in Stato e Mercato n. 5.

31. The other non-Fordist model considered by the international literature was the Japanese one that was affirming itself behind the intensive application of some microelectronic technologies (the economic growth of Japan between 1977 and 1981 was 42.3 per cent).
32. Carboni C. (1996, 1998).
33. Trigilia C. (2005), *Sviluppo locale. Un progetto per l'Italia*, Laterza, Roma-Bari.
34. Carboni C. (2005c), *Nuova economia, nuova società,* in Sociologia del Lavoro n. 98.
35. Perulli P. (2000), *La citta' delle reti. Forme di governo nel postfordismo*, Bollati Boringhieri, Torino.
36. See Crouch C., Le Galès P., Trigilia C., and Voelzkow H., *Changing Governance of Local Economies: Responses of European Local Production Systems,* Oxford University Press.
37. Nardozzi G. (2004), *Miracolo e declino, Laterza*, Bari-Roma.
38. Porter M.E. (1990), *The Competitive Advantage of Nations*, Macmillan, London.
39. Granovetter M. (1973).
40. Carboni C. (ed.) (2009), *La governance dello sviluppo locale*, Il Mulino, Bologna.
41. See Butera F., Donati E., Cesaria R. (1997), *I lavoratori della conoscenza. Quadri, middle manager e alte professionalità tra professione e organizzazione,* Franco Angeli, Milano. Reich R.B. (1993), L'economia delle nazioni, Il sole24ore, Milano.
42. In this way, reassigning importance to knowledge and skills with respect to technology, we also place ourselves in a different perspective from technological determinism, which in the years of globalization has been among the main vehicles of the single thought. Our approach is, if anything, technological constructivism.
43. Carboni C. (2002), *La nuova società: Il caso italiano*, Laterza, Roma-Bari.
44. Trigilia C. (2005).
45. Carboni C. (2007), *Elite e classi dirigenti in Italia*, Laterza, Bari-Roma.

# 2

# Ruptured Events and Social Practices in Italian Local Development

## 2.1 Local Development and the Social Rooting of the Economy

This chapter focuses on the influence that short-term socio-economic change and the innovative action of individuals and groups have exerted in the structuring dynamics of Italian local development. The choice of focus makes it possible to adopt a non-exclusively structuralist reading of these processes in order to avoid reducing the motivators of social agents and their fields of possibility to factors that the past transmits in a deterministic way to the present without individuals being able to regulate, transform or abandon them (e.g. the long historical continuity of institutional factors). On the contrary, considering change and innovation as ingredients that activate economic cultures and new forms of mobilization allows us to look at the motivational schemes of action also as a product of social practices operating in a historical timeframe. Under such a perspective, the configurations of institutional processes, although articulated in a *longue durée* of history, are influenced by particular events and ruptures in continuity. These impress specific trajectories of social and economic structuring in the contexts in which they occur. In the case of local development, at least three can be identified: 1) the two world wars; 2) the slow but inexorable collapse of the Apennine economies; 3) the advent of new collective cultural frameworks drawn up by mass media and the consumer market. All these have significantly affected entrepreneurial attitudes and syndromes, the governing cultures of local ruling classes, the social forms of collective mobilization of territories and of communities and the articulation of their class structure. On the methodological level, considering the role of historical ruptured events to be relevant makes it possible to loosen structuralist constructive constraints. In other words, introducing into the "genealogy" of local development the change and innovation of social practices avoids reducing individual and collective action to a flow of possibilities contained in cultural matrices that cannot be influenced by social actors.

To outline the set of themes that we will discuss in the course of this work, it is appropriate to start from the paradigm of New Economic Sociology, i.e. the theory of the social rooting of economic processes. According to this approach, the organizational forms of economic activities depend on the historical-social contexts in which the actors and institutions that produce them operate. This theory has had the undoubted merit of re-positioning the market and its activities of exchange and production in the historical field of human, cultural and political relations.[1] The concept of embeddedness criticizes the political economy for the abstract mechanics with which it defines social action and for the atomization of its agents. *Homo economicus* is, indeed, an agent indifferent to his historical and cultural context and guided by instrumental intentionality regulated by a natural aptitude to adopt rational solutions and choices. There are two immediate consequences to such reasoning. On the one hand, selfishness becomes the optimizer of economic behaviour, on the other, social action is pulverized in a semi-neutral context of institutions aimed at transmitting information on goods and prices. These are the mechanisms that the equations of market equilibrium theories have tried, with varying success, to measure in order to explain the "physics of the economy". If the latter were to translate its assumptions into the concrete reality of everyday life, we would find ourselves faced with an unrecognizable world. Let us begin with optimizing selfishness. Human individuals have characteristics of aggression and selfishness, but their species reproduction implies eusocial behaviours. Human evolution as a eusocial process shifts the focus from the theory of kinship genetic selfishness (i.e. the selfish gene) to the new perspective of group selection.[2] This argument provides explanations of human altruism as oriented by cooperation, mutual support and solidarity. Not the selfish gene but rather the defence of the nest seems to be the reproductive motive of men, and this practice ends up ordering at a phenotypic level our specific social inclinations aimed at encountering the Other and at cooperation. At the same time, placing human action in the neutral producer information market, endowed with a physiological capacity for self-regulation, reduces human choices to the pure objective calculability of preferences. This assumption, if it is adequate for the criteria of explanation of methodological reductionism, in which the social and emotional nature of individuals and institutions is removed, conflicts with the fact that human actions and preference structures respond to specific "frameworks of morality" that are historically determined and subject to mutation.[3]

On the basis of such critical arguments, it is necessary to understand why the empirical limit of the economic actor is not taken so seriously. The answer to the question and the logical problem that derives from it must be traced in the epistemology of the social sciences. Its theories and various disciplinary fields have indeed recognized the field of action of the "human subject" not so much in empirical adherence to its historical-social concreteness, but rather in the methodological constraints identified by each theoretical and disciplinary corpus.[4] Political economy is not exempt from this predicament; there is no individual who responds to the constraints of choice of *homo economicus*, and the disappearance of social and political influences in the determination of those constraints is counter intuitive. Such descriptive restrictions on human inclinations and the social fields in which they are formed, distributed and exchanged have given us an image of the market as a material space for point-like individuals.[5] These are projected towards a future without direction that does not contemplate history and conceives the present as a continuous fabric of choices guided by calculative rationality. On the one hand, the latter neutralizes every emotional basis of social choices and relationships, on the other, it renders as pure superstition any hypothesis that the images and perceptions of the real world depend on collective representations.[6]

The theories of the social rooting of the economy try to respond to all these "empirical restrictions" of human institutional action. Contextually, however, they produce contradictions that are still challenging to resolve. For example, institutions themselves, in the long period of their structuring, end up "neutralizing" in a matrix of continuity the role of politics, historical events and collective practices. In the case of Italian local development, this has resulted in the underestimation of both social change caused by historical rupture events and the processes of modernization and their transforming impact on behaviours and social, cultural, psychological relationships, as well as those of meaning. In reality, and such is the interpretative hypothesis of this work, the economic structuring of local development, beyond historical-anthropological factors (social organization of family models, land possession systems, etc.), has been influenced by symbolic universes of reality of a hedonic type (e.g. consumerism and new aesthetic meanings) that have articulated psychological images of desire and trajectories of social action, generating new forms of legitimization and the recognition of actors.[7]

The first theme bound to this way of reading development processes is that of change, which, in the long duration of the effects of social rooting on the economy seems to give way to continuity. Contextually, social structures appear to overpower social practices, reducing individuals to pure institutionalized agents. Finally, market modernization, rather than as a cultural and psychological device of the ethical and behavioural transformation of traditional values and obligations, is delineated as a background in which local societies and their hyper-institutionalized actors acquire a specific "identity resistant to the mutation of deep cultures". This is possible assuming that structural factors and values of tradition can operate in terms of selective continuity, becoming functional to productive and social innovation triggered by industrial modernization. Thus, arguing instead of reading the tensions of change that operate in the encounters between tradition and innovation, the latter express an active balance of continuity.

## 2.2 Modernization and Local Development: A Difficult Relationship

The underestimation of modernization, of its commodified cultures and hedonistic psychologies and of the individualization of society has generated a (cultural-institutional) vision of local development according to which some pre-capitalist continuities, such as the extended and complex productive family, the sharecropping land possession system and widespread forms of self-consumption (informal economy), allowed functional integration in these territories of the ethical characteristics of productive mobilization and of labour imposed by the industrial revolution. This specificity allowed the activation of market dynamics in the regulation of labour relations. Widely distributed low wages and wage and consumption supplements through informal economies met a disciplined labour force and a fabric of distinctly enterprising and sufficiently organized small-scale entrepreneurs. Both social forces of the new local industrial model were ethical legacies of the sharecropping rationalization of agricultural activities.[8]

This paradigm has privileged a description of the development wherein modernization, rather than a force of transformation, was a background from which local communities could trace out tangible identity boundaries. This placed them along a continuum that rooted the market and industrial economy in pre-capitalistic cultural and value systems. This rooting of economic institutions has exclusively determined the structuring effect of the social context on how resources are organized and distributed. If, on the one hand, this criterion for explaining development has allowed the highlighting of the geographical and social diversity of institutional factors, on the other, it has imprisoned them in a historical-cultural furrow with unsurpassable borders. A fundamental assumption with which New Economic Sociology argues the dynamics of development is that of the variety of capitalisms (Burroni, 2016).[9] There are various capitalisms, various ways of organizing industrial production or the consumption and welfare system, according to the effects of path dependence on the institutionalization processes of economic forms. A different way of organizing family relationships, obligations and hereditary mechanisms might explain the diversity of Anglo-Saxon and Germanic-Japanese capitalisms, such as the advent of a widespread industrialization system or its failure to emerge.[10]

Folded on the dynamics of local Italian development, the selective continuity of institutional factors outlined here implies that industry and modernization, far from supplanting the rural socio-economic system, have spread over it, creating an institutional and cultural continuity between frameworks of tradition (extended family, sharecropping, etc.) and modernity.

The metal labourer, the mobilized family and a self-disciplined labour force were the arranged combinations of a nascent industrial and consumer development based on "country economies". This vision is the emblem with which local development territories and their communities have established and legitimated their own value systems, fuelling questions of social, economic and political autonomy.[11] This narrative of the industrialization of the centre-north-east of the country has supported several processes: 1) the emergence of a sense of identity and belonging to the local context emancipated from the rural minority (the local community); 2) the affirmation of new collective actors capable of generating additional wealth and social cohesion (local entrepreneurs); 3) the formation of a demand for recognition of those communities and regional areas as economic, social and cultural fields in search of political autonomy (local governance of the territorial development).

The international opening of these territories, communities and economic-industrial systems, however, has exposed many limitations of the mainstream vision of Italian local development. The look at the present offered in previous chapters, rather than the long continuity and selective accumulation of institutional factors, evidences disjointed territorial areas. There has been, on the one hand, the consolidation of several innovative industrial groups, on the other, the disintegration of many SME productive chains left at the behest of organizational and technological innovation, and, in the middle, social fabrics profoundly transformed by the capitalist and industrial cycle of the last two decades. This has led to unemployment, stagnation and social disorientation for an economy and a collective life in apparent decline and marked by a new ethnic and demographic geography of the old local communities.[12]

In our opinion, local development is no longer identifiable with the institutional uniformity that had characterized the prevailing narrative of territorial production models. Such diffusive, imitative and self-propulsive homogeneity of development, an aspect on which Italian industrial communities had built their visibility and their economic-political autonomy, appears to be particularly articulated. The crisis, which is slowly being surmounted, as well as showing the force of contingent events on the continuity of the long period, has highlighted how the economy of districts is no longer a homogeneous and functionally differentiated set of technical configurations of production. On the contrary, it presents itself as a territorial milieu where the factors of innovative institutional culture and technological research make the difference. In this sense, the socio-territorial differentiation in the capacity of Italian local systems to react proactively to the crisis of the last decade is symptomatic of structural in homogeneities between regions and territories and consequently of different performance capacities on the economic and political-regulatory plane. This has entailed, for local development areas, an internal re-hierarchization with economies that have assumed different speeds, determining a split between those that held onto the continental platform of the European economy (Emilia-Romagna and Veneto), those that now represent a periphery (Marche and Umbria) and those, such as Tuscany, that hover between the two poles without constituting a possible bridging.

Even the supposed balance between tradition and modernity seems definitively altered by economic and cultural globalization and local life appears redefined by the absorption of distant and universalizing influences (Giddens, 1994).Among these, market and media relations have unified many social fields in which a multicultural multitude is expressed in search of identity and recognition. This can happen through access to new consumption and to new civil and human rights, or through migrations that rewrite the social, human and political geography of the many world communities that today inhabit the planetary scene.

The issues described allow a qualification of our hypothesis according to which the effect of modernization on local development has, at least, been sweetened. Four elements can aid in understanding this: 1) the way in which the role of the sharecropping family has been narrated; 2) the mythopoesis of the local entrepreneur; 3) the underestimation of consumption in the action strategies of individuals and social classes; 4) the absence of the city from development models of small and medium-scale family businesses.

In the mainstream model, the family is narrated as a unit of production in a specificera, that of Italian industrialization, which, as in other Western developed countries, had long since expelled the family from the sphere of production to reposition it in that of consumption. Already in the 1970s, the Italian urban middle classes seemed to be engaged in a cultural and economic process of transformation of the home into a domestic space with low intensity of symbolic commitments towards public regulatory conformity. Work, income and, above all, mass consumption privatized many areas of legitimization and the social self-fulfilment of individuals (process of subjectification). The family assumed the connotations of a self-referential social unit, which concentrated its affective, cultural, moral, economic and political choices "inside the home", accessing industrially produced symbols, status, information and values. The latter took on the sense of emblems necessary to legitimize personal identities in the new social fields delineated by modernization. Thus the home became the main area of formation of the social character of Italian consumers. While the home and the family, as a unit of production, typical of a rural economy, are significantly open and exposed to the external constraints of legitimization and the recognition of social obligations, implying a strong social bond with the community and public life, the home, as a unit of consumption, typical of market societies, presents itself as a privatized space, typical of an individualized society regulated by hedonic ethics and practices of recognition and legitimization of an aesthetic nature. The home unit of modern domesticity becomes the symbolic field where the family finds the configurations of compromise between affective economies within the nucleus and demands for recognition and participation in public life. This implies a flow of social exchange that underlines how mass consumption has transformed the symbolic universes and economic structures of individuals and social contexts. Individualization and commodification of life spaces are the main dynamics triggered by this long-term transformation, which also in the case of local Italian development is attributable to the process that Lipotvesky has defined as the "second individualist revolution". This is characterized by total individualism freed from subjection to moral rules and traditional community anchorages.[13]

In the mainstream model of local development, the entrepreneur is narrated as the specific product of a rural-sharecropping work ethic that underlines the features of continuity with pre-existing social ties and with the values of communitarian tradition. This argument once again underestimates the transforming force of market modernization. It presents the actors and the Italian companies of the economic development of the 1970s as residues in equilibrium with an extraordinary and improbable mix between tradition and innovation.

For the local entrepreneur, productive organization referred to the family structure constitutes a cultural objective, a sort of normative type that reflects specific values and traditions typical of a rural society (Blim, 1991).[14] This does not mean, however, that such a relationship exhausts the spectrum of social and economic changes triggered by territorial industrialization.

In the continuity between sharecropping and industry, the objectives of groups and classes coincide with the accumulation of resources purposed for the security of the family and with the investment of surpluses in goods of social prestige aimed at increasing the status and visibility of the family itself. The local entrepreneur transcends the merely economic dimension with objectives that are not exclusively market-oriented but reflect a typology characterized by the local lifestyle. The same workers, even if from different economic and social positions, do not appear less sensitive to the new aspirations of status triggered by the advent of industrial manufacturing. Access to modern consumption and its ostentation serve as a symbolic vehicle of redemption for a subsistence farming society now committed to positioning itself on the ladder of modernity. From the socio-cultural mix described emerges a locally shared industrial logic in which a marked individualistic opportunism corresponds to a meagre culture of social planning. The public ethic of commitment to community needs is often instrumental in reflecting a paternalistic social role that elevates reputation. Contextually, the entrepreneur is engaged in a symbolic battle of self-recognition based on the pursuit of the distinctive statuses of the wealthy class. Conspicuous consumption and economic waste, for its own sake, qualify these symbolic strategies, which re-formulate, in a climate of "contradiction", the sense of pride and of social affirmation.[15] On the one hand, the "cultural prototype" of the local entrepreneur invests the wealth and materiality of success in territorial and communitarian symbolic economies (e.g. luxury villas and cars, philanthropic parish and social activities), on the other, however, his individual affirmation in those symbolic economies disqualifies him from the tradition he would like to incarnate. The objects, symbols and statuses of success and their ostentation, indeed, draw the normative force of their meaning and social recognition from bureaucratic and globalizing value structures, which those communitarian frame works localized in tradition tend to transform at a moral reference framework level.

In the mainstream model of local development, mass consumption appears to be excessively undervalued with respect to the role it plays in the strategies of action of individuals and social classes. Consumption is a component that informs the cognitive and material structure of every social system.[16] Its structuring influence depends on the normative and regulatory conformation that characterizes the sources of cultural flow. Hannerz[17] categorized four in particular: forms of life, the state, the market and social movements. Each of these is affected by different norms of regulation of social life. From this point of view, culture is an institutional product with which individuals activate a continuous process of negotiation of the meanings and principles underlying their choice of belonging to or refusal of a given framework. If, by hypothesis, we found ourselves in a social system where the sphere of daily life prevailed, the regulation of cultural flow would depend on short relational networks (e.g. clans, tribes, local communities) immersed in primary socialization contexts (i.e. proximity contacts: family-parental). The codification of the norms would be of a prevalently moral nature and would be structured on prescriptive forms handed down orally, with a strong and widespread social control in the limited sphere of proximity relations. In the same sphere, the individual dimension appears strongly compressed by social structures and by the culture of the place. On the contrary, if the market were to prevail, the relational networks would be mainly of a long type and oriented by secondary socialization contexts (e.g. specialized institutions: school, work, state, mass media; informal institutions: leisure time, friendship networks). The codification of the norms would be of an instrumental nature and their capacity to regulate would be structured through (specialized) codes legitimized by the force of law. In this context, the individual dimension is emancipated both from the cogent force of the social structures of belonging and from the local culture, no longer an identification of the type of a member of that family, belonging to that community, but a person as such. We can therefore draw a robust hypothesis around the fact that the consumer society modifies the psycho-social structures of tradition, redrawing individual self-perception and its self-understanding in the relationship with the public dimension. In other words, the individual consumer lives the community collective context as a place, among others, in which to construct his personal existential trajectory.

Finally, in the mainstream model, the city is the significant absentee in the development of small and medium-scale family businesses. This social and economic aggregation of capitalist rationalization and modernization is subordinated to the local development systems, understood as productive communities spread along territorial continuums that trace, and transform, the physical and social geography of the preceding agricultural model. The valley lines along the interior to coast main routes thus become the urbanized countryside that is gradually integrated by infrastructural coalescence into the urban areas of first urbanization.[18]

The privileged territorial unity that emerges from such considerations is the industrial district, a container of development and social relations that, more than any other, was associated with a predominantly economic and productive vision of the territory. In some respects, cities, even though they have been important irradiation centres for the launching of local development, incubating artisan networks and activating the first outlet markets, always appeared external to the codified boundaries of disciplinary analyses. This undervaluation seems surpassed today, with the city recognized as having a much more incisive role in local development, and this recognition is all the more significant the more district economies have reconverted their organizational and productive forms under the pressure of a pervasive outsourcing of their activities. The emergence of local services economies has therefore re-centred the development scenarios within city fabrics, privileged meeting points for the presence of private and public tertiary activities.[19]

## 2.3 Economy and Society: Social Capital and Trust

### *2.3.1 The Collective Dimension*

The social structuring of the economy looks towards the continuity and selective accumulation of institutional factors, as well as the long-term effect of socio-cultural foundations on the performance of a context. An example of this is the social capital of Putnam, a product of civism and of the associative predisposition of a territory.[20] According to this well-known perspective, during the last eight centuries, the various logics of the political and social systems of central-northern Italy, characterized by the local autonomies of municipalities and seigniories, and southern Italy, characterized by dependence on foreign dominions, have formed their current structures with a continuity of cause and action that neither the regulatory action of politics nor the innovative action of economic actors have influenced. While the south develops vertical and self-referential cultures of government, the centre-north is characterized by horizontality and greater democratic and participatory openness. The explanation of the differentials of social capital between the two areas, however, overshadows a "philosophy of history" by which social facts occur as products determined by the action of the past on the present. The functional or dysfunctional aspects of a social-historical order consistently impose solutions of continuity, which, whether virtuous, or persistently defective, are forever unable to change the course of history. Collective and individual actions are thus placed in a finalistic linearity within the historical process. This means being able to read the world as a verifiable series of sums of events where certain winning cultural matrices determine the historical structures of societies. While Putnam's idea of looking at the history of cultural characteristics as a slow process is admissible, it is also necessary that their forms of accumulation, persistence and variation are explained and not simply proposed as factors operating in a "semi-automatic" way in undifferentiated contexts.

Several Italian scholars have been critical of this way of considering the historical processuality of institutional formation.[21] Their considerations value, together with long-period historical and cultural factors, political ones tied to particular events and emerging social actors. The Second World War, the Resistance, the collapse of rural economies and the labourer and sharecropper struggles produced social mobilization in the areas of Central-Northern Italy with profound political implications. The republican and democratic mass politics welcomed these new collective actors due to the presence of adequate local identity resources provided by networks of small towns in such areas and by their mutualistic heritage of socialist and Catholic origins. For Trigilia, this mechanism favoured the emancipation of politics from society, under a process of modernization that brought out new broader political solidarity networks, freed from traditional family ties and the particularist interests of context. The local political class thus was able to enjoy a generalized consensus that, from the narrow sphere of traditional private interests, moved towards the production and implementation of collective goods and services useful for supporting economic development. In such circumstances, the conscious action of the political class assumes a strong influence with respect to the fate of the formation and consolidation of the "de-centred" areas of Italian development.[22] A more "interventionist" role of social-communist institutions (local welfare, development support, collective goods and services production) is then matched by a less regulated local market in Catholic-Christian-Democrat areas. If the Italian Communist Party constituted the centre of gravity of a broad and yet compact associative and institutional constellation, the Christian Democrat Party developed an intervention of distributive mediation of resources between the centre and the periphery. Such arguments emphasize the influence of the political government on the mechanisms of economic development and on the formation of normative guidelines for action in civil society. The empirical concreteness of the institutional performances of local governments (e.g. Red Emilia, White Veneto and the Marche Model) evidenced that the theory of the social rooting of the economy could contemplate short-term change. This mechanism, especially in the south of Italy, could become performative provided that the local ruling classes faced up to economic stagnation with a recovery of institutional and political autonomy, especially in light of the administrative decentralization processes that were taking shape in the early 1990s (Trigilia, 1986). Political elites and ruling classes failed, however, to respond to several of the issues that this challenge imposed, not least the negotiated planning of development, because they were embroiled in localistic particularities and were unable to grasp the complexity and risks that local economies ran in facing, in spite of themselves, the global processes of the new economy. Examples come from the low effectiveness of the institutional anti-crisis measures put in place by local governments, the de-industrialization endured and badly governed and the financial crashes of many territorial financial fabrics. Looking at the present, Trigilia's formula of "development without autonomy" seems to be logically reversible: "autonomy without development", a paradox often confirmed by the lack of transparency, if not corruption, of the ruling and political classes of many local governments in a mix of self-referentiality and clientelism that has exasperated many systemic inefficiencies, generating crony capitalism and "amoral localism".[23]

### 2.3.2 The Individual Dimension

Even the micro-individual model of social capital, of which Coleman is the main exponent, poses several problems of logical and sociological consistency. Indeed, according to Coleman, social capital would consist of the complex of social relations that the individual is able to use in order to achieve his own goal.[24]

On the logical plane, the ambiguity of Coleman's definition lies in the theoretical assumptions underlying it, that is, that society consists of a set of independent individuals who act with objectives that can themselves be pursued independently. The functioning of the social system is thus embodied in the simple combination of these independent individual actions and social capital is reduced to a network of vectors that unite various points that correspond to just as many actors.[25] The normative structure, which is also considered by Coleman as a distinctive factor of social capital, ends up dissolving into an element of the network, even though it represents a substratum. This contradiction is explained by a double contingency of the model. On the one hand, social capital is presented as a characteristic of social structure, on the other, it is reduced to a simple network that connects the various independent individuals who act to achieve their own goals. What follows is a description of society as a simple sum of actors acting to achieve instrumental ends.

On the sociological plane, Coleman's approach, envisaging the instrumentality of social capital, implies an overlap between relationships economically targeted at the pursuit of instrumental objectives and relational aspects not immediately targetable (family-friendly reciprocity, education, community solidarity) (Pizzorno, 2001). From this consideration it follows that to have relationships implies an instrumental and targeted use of those relationships to raise the level of individual resources in order to produce greater wealth for the actors. In this perspective, social capital presents itself as an intentionally used resource, which implies that individual action is exercised in a context of social relations that the individual uses as means for the pursuit of certain ends. In this way, all those aspects of social capital that do not represent a useful benefit for individuals but which may have a positive effect at a wider social level, for example by raising the level of trust in a given context, are excluded. These arguments imply relevant theoretical sociological issues. In an explanation of social capital as an appropriable good for intentional individual ends, it is the method and field of action of sociology that are challenged. For Pizzorno (2001): "*It is no longer a question of reconstructing the map of social structures within which the individual forms and pursues his goals, but rather of taking these ends for granted and analysing those structures as means*". On this ground, the sociological analysis restricts social action to a predominantly rational nature of individual action, assuming an interpretative paradigm flattened to the economic dimension: actions instrumentally guided by a logic of type means-ends. If society becomes accessory to the market and is characterized by the potential of the relational action of individuals, then social capital, more than a specific object, represents "*a point of view on the totality of society, or, in any case, on a vast and not well delimitable totality of social phenomena*" (Bagnasco, 1999).

A way that tries to avoid such "explanatory absolutism" is that with which Mutti outlines the formation of trust fabrics in a context of operative "trust in change".[26] Exclusively binding trust to expectations of regularity implies excluding from the trust relationship expectations of change in the social organization and its basic rules. This ends up neglecting those mechanisms of variability and precariousness of the systemic and institutional trust that have characterized different historical-social contexts over time. For example, with respect to individual trust syndromes, the systematic connections that are traced between family models and forms of capitalism do not explain the mechanism that determines the formation of individual value orientations and the dynamics of interpersonal trust that those connections produce. This highlights the existence of a "missing link" in the logical connections that describe the macro-structural variables underlying the individual and collective trust ties. Contextually, however, there is not yet an adequate and satisfactory theory of the ways to create those bonds of trust at the micro level that are capable of ordering the value orientations of individuals. The most satisfactory scheme is that of Erikson, according to whom trust is the prerogative of individuals with greater self-esteem and trust in general (basic trust).The mature personality emerges as a positive solution to the conflict between basic trust and basic distrust, a tension that occurs especially in the first year of life of the child in the mother-child relationship. From this point of view, the way in which the trust game has been articulated within the family is fundamental for the extension of trust dynamics to extra-family contexts. Furthermore, families with models of relationships open to the outside world and with extended family relations facilitate the generalization of trust, favouring a positive-sum trust mechanism between confidence in oneself, in others and in social institutions (Mutti, 1998). In this way it is possible to integrate, on the developmental psychology plane, the structural sociological approach, by tracing in the family socialization processes the "missing link" in the macro relationship between family structure and economic and entrepreneurial development.[27]

## 2.4 Market Modernization

Regarding market modernization and the fact that its economic aspects are rooted in the social contexts of belonging or released from them, there has been an intense debate between the positions of Polanyi and Granovetter. On the one hand is the great commodifying transformation of social life that frees economic functioning from it (accessory societies), and, on the other, the influence of relational and institutional structures for economic actions (social rooting of the economy) (Steiner, 2011).[28] In general, the economy as a productive and allocative process and as a set of human activities aimed at transforming nature is unique. What makes economic forms manifold are the different regulatory systems that coordinate factors. Polanyi[29] interpreted economic systems through integration schemes. These mechanisms should not be confused with the temporal and sequential stages of development, where each stage of system evolution surpasses another that will be forgotten by history. *On the contrary, according to Polanyi, in the integration scheme of the self-regulated market, may remain as institutional forces both reciprocity and redistribution, the other two integration schemes of economic systems that have anticipated the market exchange. This "active residuality" of past institutional structures of the economy has entered the "narrative" of local development, evidencing the strategic function of informal economies in integrating into rural social contexts the productive rationality of industry and the modernization of the market.* Thus conceived, the regulatory mechanisms are socio-institutional organization systems that allow actors to circulate goods and practice exchanges. If, in the schemes of reciprocity and redistribution, economic activity is rooted in social relations (embedded), in the organization of the capitalist market, on the other hand, there is a conflict between market and society. The economy, structuring itself on the basis of the self-regulated market, therefore on the commodification of social resources, separates itself from other institutions, compelling society to function according to the laws of its organization: society transforms into an accessory component of the market. The most significant indicator of this process is the commodification of human relations, that is the goods status of the individual when he operates within the labour market, satisfies his needs through monetary exchanges and lives in ecosystems structurally functional to the dynamics of economic development.

The accessory aspect of social relations in the economic functioning of the self-regulated market is the critique motivating New Economic Sociology and its idea of the social rooting of economic relations. According to this perspective, the separation between socially rooted primitive economies and the market economy released from every aspect of social relations, does not contemplate the processuality of a series of modern economic dynamics, such as job searches, where primary social ties (family) and institutional (extra-family) persist (Granovetter, 1973). All this reveals the influence of the relational and institutional structures within which economic actions are realized and highlights how the concept of rooting offers both an original description of the social basis of economic activities and a model of social relations that allows coordination between market agents (Steiner, 2011).

This debate, however important and illustrious, presents a limit in the interpretation that both theories adopt for the historical transmission of social characteristics. This leads them to not adequately grasp what it is that changes and, above all, the quality and extent of this change. In the case of Polanyi, the advent of the market and cultural modernization changes the whole structure of social relations to the point of subsuming them into economic ones, thus describing a sort of alienated totality of capitalism. In the case of New Economic Sociology, however, the market is a social construction, a historical product of socialization and institutionalization. This way of arguing about the social formation of the economy has advantages and limitations. Among the first is the possibility of reading, in diachronic terms, the long historical duration of social structures, reconstructing the dynamics up to the stabilization of an interpretative model of the present. The concept of local development is a proficuous, dialogical and explanatory expression of it. Among other limitations is the difficulty of giving due consideration to the processes of transformation and perturbation of socio-institutional structures. This circumstance occurs when the process of socio-cultural evolution is read in cumulative terms and as "linear output", in other words, as a long continuity and homogeneity of institutional factors. Thus reasoning, socio-economic development is not influenceable by the choices of actors. On the contrary, the latter are always determined by the specific institutional context in which they operate. The dominance of social formation and its "given cultural matrix" of the possibilities of individual and collective action obscure important elements in understanding the social processes underlying the choices and economic configurations of a territory. On the one hand, there are the cultural and psychological factors that feed the local entrepreneurial fabric (motivations and individual incentives of entrepreneurial choice), on the other hand, subjective and institutional trust mechanisms, such as family ones, that explain the emergence of trust and innovative-entrepreneurial dynamics. Thus arguing, there is a tendency to value more the aspects of continuity and/or of gradual change than rupture and social innovation produced by contingent historical events. In this way, it is not possible to explain how, when and why certain subjects have become activators of development (Paci, 1999).

In reflection on the genesis of local development, an escape from this "caging" of the social construction of the economy is offered by Trigilia[30]. The author attributes to the Second World War and to the Resistance a decisive role in the formation of new collective identities. In the cultural context of many areas of local development, the new political orientations assume a tendentially communitarian character. Adhesion to a new political structure is affirmed in the first post-war phase as part of a wider reaction of local communities to the social, political and economic upheavals caused by the war. This dynamic also extends to class relations, especially in light of peasant struggles, phenomena that re-articulate social stratification and structures of traditional inequalities, preparing the way for the industrial economy. Extraordinary events, such as those described, have decisively influenced the lines of transformation of the social life of a new generation, breaking a class structure handed down by the rural tradition (Paci, 1999).All this makes it legitimate to ask whether the historical origins of innovative and entrepreneurial syndromes should not be sought precisely in those events, rather than in the institutional continuity of socio-cultural structures. The War, the Resistance, peasant struggles and emigration related to the collapse of mountain and foothill economies transformed the collective imagination of entire generations, producing a vast social mobilization and a rapid process of cultural and economic modernization. The culture of work and the proto-entrepreneurial inclinations of sharecroppers expressed their potential thanks to the political and social conjuncture and the favourable economic phase that opened up in the immediate post-war period. All this invites us to evaluate, in the emergence of interpersonal trust dynamics that favour the formation of entrepreneurship, the influence of social and cultural continuity elements, typical of traditional agrarian structures, and of moments of rupture of such structures. The modernization of local development territories and communities can be interpreted, on the one hand, as a gradual process of functional adaptation of cultural and social elements of tradition to the new "industrial regime", on the other, as the outcome of events occurring in a specific historic moment. The latter are relatively rare events that do not reproduce social structures but change them significantly. They do not, however, transform history into an indistinct flow of changes but consider it the product of regularity and ruptures, where social change is a emergence left relatively easy to interpret.[31]

## 2.5 Cultures of Consumption and Local Development

In the last two decades, especially among economics historians, many authors have highlighted the importance of the consumer revolution and the influence it has exerted on the industrial one of the late eighteenth century.[32] The cultures of consumption, the symbolic spaces occupied by groups that compete in the sphere of material interests, have redesigned European and global socio-economic scenarios.

Economics and culture are expressions of a single flow that mixes symbolic values and exchange values from life with social formations and their structures of reproductive organization. In interacting and considering the relationship between culture and economic processes, there are different and contrasting interpretative social sciences paradigms. There is the structuralist model, which, by reducing culture to a deterministic and unconscious matrix of patterns of social action, considers individuals "machines of procedural execution". At the other end of the spectrum, there are those who think of culture as the symbolic fabric of the signification of reality, constructivism, social phenomenology, symbolic interactionism, seeing in the schemes of individual action and in language the only objects relevant to the social sciences. The structuralist model removes individuals in favour of institutional processes in which their action unfolds. The constructivist one conceives reality as a socially symbolized subjective product. The result is the impossibility of synthesis and reciprocal enclosure within well-defined boundaries. This separation has not produced synergistic results that would otherwise be possible by holding the two paradigms in a complementary and flow relationship, thinking of culture as a both a structural and constructivist process. It would thus be possible to consider, in the explanation of the relationship between society and the individual, both the influence of the structures on the potential fields of action and of the subjective ability to incorporate inherited culture into an original and personal form, that is to transform and adapt it, through specific intentional practices, to tackle the problems to be solved and the objectives to be achieved in a certain course of history. This means to unite, as Braudel would say, both the slow flow of a river, given by the continuous structure of its course, and its surface ripples, sudden, changeable and able to impact, in some cases also quite significantly, the apparent continuity of the flow.

How can we account for the complementarity between social structures and individual practices that we have highlighted and the biunivocity with which they determine the structuring of social organizations? First of all, let us start with a specification of human relationships that are, at the same time, relationships of strength and meaning. The symbolic concerns the sphere of the subjective, the sphere of power relations concerns the objective order where structural dynamics operate independently from the wills and representations of social actors. This line of reasoning tells us that individuals can construct social phenomena through their thinking and acting, but such construction always takes place within a structure that can never be removed. Therefore transformations are possible not in spite of the "dominion of the structures" but on the basis of its persistence, which is a necessary condition for socialization itself. This is the theoretical basis of the "duality of structure".[33] Social action, based on the conscious self, or performing self, is made up of desired (strategic) effects that develop other undesired effects not contemplated by initial objectives. Just think of the use of our mother tongue (structure); when we speak it, we implicitly draw upon its grammatical rules and, in doing so, we reproduce the language itself without meaning to it. But languages are never equal to themselves, they change over time, while still maintaining underlying structural rules. It is under this perspective that we can imagine the transformation process that springs from the indissoluble bond between action and social structures.

The duality of structure represents both a limitation to the possibilities of agency and the field in which it can select its possibilities.[34] This complementary mechanism is the engine of social structuring, that set of cultural patterns and social resources for which each structure represents together the means and the outcome of the practices of social systems, that is to say, of human actions (Giddens, 1984; Sewell, 2008). This reasoning makes it possible to consider the interpretation of social phenomena also through the instrument of semiosis, that is the production of the frames of meaning within which decisions, calculations and perception of structural constraints are generated. This crucial force of semiotic codes exhausts neither social life nor the tools of social analysis. Social life is not reduced to a play of meanings or to a pure interpretable linguistic text. On the contrary, society is representable as a network of semiotic practices within a "constructed environment". This is the material, geographic and architectural infrastructure of collective life, in which significant practices constitute and change physical frameworks, which, in turn, are the matrices of those practices and conductors of their effects.[35] The symbolic practices and capacities that express them are instruments that allow the production of fields of reality, spaces of meaning within which is articulated the coordinated process of social life and of the existential truths that legitimize it. Existential truths are naturalized bases of meaning, the obvious aspects of common sense, representations of the world that have become objective foundations of our perceptive and action field. Such objectification makes it different from us. Social institutions are this, symbolic realities that we have created but which also appear to us separate, pre-existing and to which we adapt our behaviour.[36] The relationships between the individual and society are of this type, expressing a complementarity where collective representations generate collective consciences to which individuals adhere unconsciously. From this adhesion derives the possibility of an extended symbolic exchange that is implemented with practices and strategies that, in turn, contribute to building new possibilities for social action.

According to this reasoning, the social actors, protagonists of local development, and the motivation systems that have led them to innovate customs and behaviours are placed within a historical-social framework fuelled by three major events: the Second World War, the definitive collapse of the Apennine economies and the long wave of the economic boom. The latter has realized a pervasive consumer economy, transforming, in a sudden and profound way, popular Italian culture, commercializing it in the pursuit of status and social times. The protagonists of this transformation were the middle classes, broad entrepreneurship and a new working class with strong aspirations for integration in the world of widespread prosperity.[37]

The social and cultural modernization of consumption has generated ethical and value transformations that have favoured and diversified the inclination towards entrepreneurial risk, fuelling changes in social, psychological and value behaviour in vast components of the social structure. As Castronovo suggests,[38] both the economic boom and consumer culture came as an unexpected surprise in Italian public debate. The political and economic ruling classes did not grasp what people had been practicing for some time. They did not perceive the link between the productive and distributive innovation of resources and cultural modernization, a synergy that suddenly left behind the old rural structure of the country. In other words, the reception of consumerist culture anticipated its rationalized understanding. With their practices of experimenting with new lifestyles, entrepreneurs and consumers anticipated social scientists, intellectuals and ruling classes in understanding the novelties and opportunities that history offered.

The individual liberation of destinies related to market culture silently disrupted the age-old forms of social obligation and the frugalism that characterized rural societies (of the deep countryside). At the same time it left behind in history the petty-bourgeois parsimony consolidated from the unitary period up to fascism among office workers, small-scale autonomous producers and the popular classes of the cities (Asquer, 2011). These new possibilities of action and social identity ripened out of the social obligations of the old traditions.

In many ways, consumerism began to be discussed after ex post facto. Even Pasolini, who was among the very first to denounce several of its contradictions, spoke of it in the past tense, as a market-based acculturation of Italians so sudden and pervasive as to be invisible to the eyes of critics.[39] In very few years, a long history had been changed, and during the economic boom both hegemonic political cultures in the country were not equipped to adequately understand or govern the ongoing transformation. Consumerism entered into the practices of Italians and their culture without a real collective discourse, and neither critical nor enthusiastic. Everything was left to the new media and symbolic grammars of the television and commercial complex. TV and places of consumption educated the new Italians, "spoiling them" with the usual stories of old.

The media culture with which mass consumption affirmed itself in Italy must make us reflect on the cultural flow that has legitimized and consolidated it over time. The channels with which messages and ideas are distributed and the psychological aspects involved in the way in which they are accessed and received are decisive in an understanding of the formation of cultures and orientations of social and economic behaviour. For example, romantic poetry and the gothic novel contributed to the development of a romantic ethic of consumption based on the hedonism of the senses in Europe.[40] The aesthete in front of a work of art is the prototype of this circumstance. We are thus in the presence of a still highly self-directed individual, whose modalities of cultural reception draw from the aesthetic fields of the novel, of poetry, of art.[41]

Things changed with the assertion of the self-illusory hedonist desire, a modality in which the subject is gradually shifted from a self-directed model of receiving cultural, physical and psychological stimuli to a direct other, in which pleasure coincides more with wanting than with having. In such circumstance, the individual imagination of a possible "social self" (roles, status, etc.) may form through daydreaming or reverie.[42]

While in traditional (self-directed) hedonism we want what is known and has been experienced in the past, in modern hedonism (other-directed) the tendency to resort to the imagination to perfect pleasures and project them forwards to a future experience tends to focus desire on things of which no experience has been had. Objects are cloaked by an illusory magic that makes them coincide with our dreams. In this way, through a vague and stimulated search by the imagination for an unknown object of desire, it is possible to believe in the reality of those objects before discovering concretely what they correspond to.

Social practices, cultures of consumption and collective ways of perceiving oneself (social imaginaries) are symbolic aspects that exert considerable influence with respect to the capacity of a territorial community to mobilize itself on the economic and social plane. Looking at the present, in the territories of local development, the symbolic force of local culture appears to be weakened. Labour ethics and consumer aesthetics have mingled, mutating cultural orientations and behavioural dispositions of individuals and generations.

This process, together with the disarticulation of industrial districts and the creeping economic crises of the last two decades, has worn out the symbolic force of the typified actors of development (the local entrepreneur and the metal labourer), giving way to a disenchantment, in part responsible for the cultural disorientation generated from the relationship of force between global economic and labour action and local identity. The identity emblem of "small is beautiful" appears faded in the narrative rhetoric of local systems in economic and cultural crisis. As we have repeatedly pointed out, the theories of local development have produced a widely shared system of ideas (narration) according to which tradition and innovation might have been the expression of an active balance, of a Weberian elective affinity that found incarnation in the territories of the Third Italy. In this ideological construction, the most important role was represented by the extended family of sharecropper nature, which, with an age-old vocation as a productive unit (already partly rationalized), had generated and facilitated a widespread entrepreneurial vocation, on the one hand, and a reservoir of disciplined labour, on the other, thus crucial social resources to efficiently and effectively mould the background of ongoing modernization.

This typified model has become an existential truth for political institutions, ruling classes, productive classes, citizens and workers. Like any existential truth, however, it is based on the "unsaid", it tells us a story of conventional utility, like the Baruya people who believed that the sweet potato had been cultivated in their territories since the dawn of time, ignorant of the fact that the tuber had been imported to Papua New Guinea by Europeans as late as the sixteenth century.

The self-perception of a community concerns the ordering of its existential truths. These are symbolic forms of recognition and legitimization of the fabrics of everyday meaning that respond to structural mechanisms, such as unconscious determinations and culturally inherited dispositions (habitus), and to practical (operative/relational) mechanisms, in which the uses of those truths are fashioned by linguistic games, strategies of integration, syncretism and common sense.

With respect to the individual and collective representations that these produce and reproduce, the existential truths are both the result of the historical accumulation of culturally inherited institutional factors and that of the daily modalities with which social action takes place in the perceptual and meaning flow of material reality. This circumstance implies, for each individual, a minimum and a maximum of adaptation from the routine to creativity. Such boundaries of integration respond both to the impulses with which structures produce the individual sense of action and favour the material reproduction of the social system, and to the individual strategies that produce social life: those practical and alternative ways of meaning that cultural customs render flows of change in continuous pursuit of equilibrium.

A good example for understanding this dynamic is provided by the mobilization of the Italian middle classes,[43] achieved thanks to the relative advantages that they acquired in the immediate post-war period, through the democratic representation of interests with, for example, protections, redistributive reward systems, low taxation and ease of licence concessions. Thus, some typologies of independent social classes, in decline in the countries of early industrialization, were maintained, or even encouraged to grow, such as artisans, farmers and traders. In this way, the engine of diffusive development was fuelled by "incentive inequalities", social costs and opportunities that could limit, even in critical situations, dissatisfaction and dissent. The individualistic mobilization for participation in the benefits of the system found three outlets; access to the productive sphere (self-employment), access to mass consumption and leisure (privacy and free time) and the pursuit of a satisfactory social position (self-realization of the self). The acceptance of the "commodifying" culture in the local communities was possible due to the diffusion of such broad economic citizenship combined with the compensatory function of the family (multi income; self-consumption; protection networks).In so doing, politics achieved an acceptable social cohesion but with particularly high collective costs in terms of the efficiency of the national system. This underlines both regulatory, redistributive and infrastructural aspects with which public leverage influenced the emergence of local economic fabrics and the emergence of new cultural referents (media acculturation) in support of the new cultures of consumption.

Local entrepreneurial training can also be placed in the flow described above. Widespread entrepreneurship marked the entry of new collective actors in the economic, social and political field, a transformation that generated and legitimized new behavioural orientations of action, under the incitement of institutional forces such as the state and the market.

The interpretation described so far of the relationship between economy and culture and between market and society leads to the consideration of the entrepreneur of local development as an individual who, in the materiality of his present, in addition to his rural and sharecropping ethical heritage, brought with him the re-invention of the latter produced by the modernizing rationalization of economic behaviours, of psychological, religious and reproductive inclinations, of identities and of "aestheticizations" of living generated by a market society that had been consolidating itself in Italy for two decades.[44] The local entrepreneur thus establishes himself as the agent of a process of rupture with the pre-existing social order. This "original fracture" is also the result of the acculturation of the market of the Italian people, which occurred abruptly and with modalities that were destructive to the preceding social, cultural and religious order. This market acculturation took place through the continuous and direct contact of the local community and its innovation pioneers with a technocratic (commercial and mass media) culture, producer of symbolic meanings and of values and psychological mutations. Exposure to the commercial and mass media device produced new perceptive fields, generating new ways of connecting the sense of individual and collective action. All this radically transformed the perception and self-realization of the self, and the communitarian identity that readjusted part of its traditional values to the new historical field of its potentialities, i.e. widespread industrialization. Such material and identity remixing tells us two things. The first is that entrepreneurs and local communities of local development "tamed" in some way this ethical, value and psychological torsion of their cultural specificities. One example is the configuration of the family as a regulator of last resort in industrial relations. The second is that this characteristic of adaptive dynamism is not the product of a deterministic matrix of the social rooting of the economy. On the contrary, the pre-capitalist persistences and the cultural dispositions of its social actors (habitus) represent the feedback that the local (colonized) culture has expressed in relation to the market (colonizing) one. The process of acculturation is not univocal. The civilization that imposes its own culture is also modified by the characteristics of the culture with which it comes into contact, even if the latter, when revoked, is a mere re-invention.[45] The market is not simply a regulatory institution of work, income, production and consumption that local social culture can functionally integrate into its traditional values and relational structures, but a real cultural machine that imposes its symbolic and material logic deep within the ontologies and perceptive fields of individuals, radically modifying ways of orienting action and legitimizing social life.

## REFERENCES

1. The theory of the social rooting of the economy (embeddedness) rejects the theory of rational choice, which presupposes the absolute and economic rationality of actors and their social atomization. Embeddedness, on the contrary, highlights the incorporation of the market in social institutions. This way of interpreting the dynamics of socio-economic relationships pays great attention to the role of ties between parties. Strong ties represent connections in which economic actors enjoy strong trust, a sense of collaboration and respect for partners. Weak ties, however, do not imply strong values, even if the latter are productive in

establishing collaborative relationships. Granovetter M. (1973), The Strength of Weak Ties, in *American Journal of Sociology*, 78, pp. 1360-1380. Swedberg R. (1999), *La nuova sociologia economica. Bilancio e prospettive*, Sociologia del lavoro, n. 73.

2. Wilson E.O. (2012), *The Social Conquest of Earth*, Liveright Pub Corp. For an interesting discussion of this work, see the review by Fagan P. available online at https://pierluigifagan.wordpress.com/2014/10/13/dal-gene-al-genere/.
3. In Taylor C. (1989), *Sources of the Self. The Making of the Modern Identity*, Harvard University Press., intentions, desires, inclinations and goals free human behaviour from objective causality. Among such subjective elements are also absolute goods (hyper-goods), those goods of a higher level that become sources of orientation of human actions, representing the point of view from which the other goods are evaluated, judged and chosen (moral reference frameworks). Hyper-goods have the power to conduct the normative structure of human action towards specific ideas of good, connecting individual activities and discerning among them those to be deemed socially acceptable and those not. The configurations with which a society considers good and evil, selfishness and altruism, trust and betrayal and family and community represent just such moral reference frameworks. For Taylor, these are never definitive and are destined to be historically surpassed. This means that different cultures correspond to different historical paths and reference frameworks. Sollazzo F. (2007), I principi del comunitarismo, Taylor C. and MacIntyre A., *Prospettiva Persona*, No. 61/62.
4. According to Elias, the multiple difficulties of communication between representatives of the different social and human sciences derive from a still unresolved question. Specialists of the "human universe" construct human unitary models by means of a limited segment of human beings that are subject to their observation. This implies an overly limited empirical basis of the subject agent. Homo economicus, psychoanalyticus and sociologicus are limited and conditioned by the fact that their human universe, determined by political economy, psychology and sociology and

their professional interests, becomes the arbitrary background in which every particular discipline places, defines and proposes the individual. At the same time, the components that are foreign to each disciplinary field are usually considered as elements of an unstructured background. Elias N., Goudsblom J., Mennell S. (2001), *Tappe di una ricerca*, Il Mulino, Bologna, 2001.

5. For Taylor (1989), there are as many cultural identities as value paradigms and each one is in continuous movement under the pressure of its past history, tradition and contingent factors that will modify it in the future. The Lockean point-like ego that defines the agent of individualistic-liberal theories, that which declares its independence and supremacy with respect to the social collectivity is therefore the expression of a certain reference framework, which, from Descartes, influenced Enlightenment philosophies and imposed itself in modernity as a paradigmatic reference to the individualistic nature of the social. For Taylor, social and individual pathologies, the loss of the referents of the action and the lack of any confidence in progress are the symptoms of the crisis and of the historical exhaustion of a reference framework. Faced with this junction, we must develop a moral ontology that can define hyper-goods as moral values, a task which, in modernity, has been disregarded and replaced by the practical one of establishing what is right to do. Indeed, for contemporary philosophy, morality is not important in itself, but only in relation to facts: what is right to do drowns out what is good to be. Consequently, the dominant objective of moral theory lies in the content of obligation, not in the nature of a good life (moral of obligation).
6. According to Touraine A. (1995), *Critique of Modernity*, Blackwell Pub, modernization is a massive process of subjectivation which aims at affirming the subject in a historical context in which the democratization of democracy takes shape. The post-industrial society, which is also characterized by a broad process of diversification of individual roles and collective memberships, has historically been consolidated as a programmed society where social production is a social custom not so much of technology

but of mass diffusion of representations, information and languages. Modernization metaphorically rewrites the book of the world, creates scenarios of meaning in which aesthetic fields become vehicles of economic valorisation and identity meanings (status symbols) of recognition and social contraposition. This process feeds the transformation of the relational environments in which individuals and groups meet, and such transformation is characterized by the historical growth of technical mediation environments, or by the routine incorporation of apparatuses aimed at forming and legitimating social universals of meaning, or by producing a common sense of reality. Friedman G. (1966), *Sept erudes sur l'homme e la technique*, Sociéte Nouvelle des Editions Gontheir, Paris.

7. Human and social consciousness consistently has an intentional character, directed towards objects and always aware of something. Objects present themselves to consciousness as belonging to different spheres of reality. Among these spheres of reality, there is one that has a dominant role: the reality of everyday life, which the conscience perceives in order as pre-existent, inter-subjective and self-evident. In such an operational context of socialization, the processes of preservation of the cultural order are possible through mechanisms of legitimization, among which symbolic universes are particularly important. The symbolic universe transcends the reality of everyday life and integrates different realities and institutional segments. Among the symbolic universes of reality, religion is one of the most important and enduring. The symbolic and material strategies of consumerism, for example, have produced in consumers a re-enchantment played on the penetration of the profane (consumption) within the sphere of the sacred (religion). All this is in order to legitimize the commercial regime and logic of the reality of our time. In this regard, see Ritzer's concept of "Cathedrals of Consumption," Ritzer G. (1999), *Enchanting a Disenchanted World: Continuity and Change in the Cathedrals of Consumption,* Sage Publications. Ultimately, only with the social production of symbolic universes of reality does individual identity, fundamentally precarious, receive a

certain coherence and stability. For a discussion of this approach in the sociology of knowledge, see Berger P.L. and Luckmann T. (1967), *The Social Construction of Reality*, Penguin, London.

8. Bagnasco A. (1977), *Tre Italie. La problematica territoriale dello sviluppo italiano*, Mulino, Bologna; Paci M. (1980) (ed.), *Famiglia e mercato del lavoro in una economia periferica*, Franco Angeli, Milan, 1980. Anselmi S. (2001), *Agricoltura e mondocontadino*, Il Mulino, Bologna.
9. Burroni L. (2016), *Capitalismi a confronto*, Il Mulino, Bologna.
10. Laslett P. (1972), *Household and Family in Past Times*, Cambridge University Press; Laslett P. (1977), *Family Life and Illicit Love in Earlier Generations*, Cambridge University Press; Todd E. (1998) *L'Illusion* économique. *Essai sur la stagnation des sociétés développées*, Paris, Gallimard.
11. According to Giddens, "tradition is repetition". This implies systems of truth opposed to those of rational research, showing traits in common with the psychology of compulsion. Just as, in the individual, that which is repressed can influence psychic life, so too, in societies, tradition continues to shape attitudes without awareness of it. "The past continues to live, but rather than being actively reconstructed according to tradition, it tends to dominate the action in an almost casual way. Compulsion, when it is socially generated, is in fact a tradition without traditionalism, a repetition that impedes autonomy rather than favouring it." Beck U., Giddens A., Lash S. (1994), *Reflexive Modernization*, Polity Press Blackwell.
12. Orazi F. (2011), *Le nuove comunità dello sviluppo locale*, ESI, Napoli.
13. Lipotvesky G. (1983 ), *L'*ère *du vide*, Gallimard, Paris.
14. Blim M.L. (1991), *Searching for the Small and Beautiful: Labor Process and Class Formation in the Industrialization of a Central Italian Shoe Town 1881-1985,* Ann Arbor University.
15. Veblen, T. (1953), *The Theory of the Leisure Class: An Economic Study of Institutions,* The Macmillan Company, New York.

16. Douglas M., Isherwood B. (1979), *The World of Goods,* Routledge, London.
17. Hannerz U. (1993), *Cultural Complexity: Studies in the Social Organization of Meaning*, Columbia University Press.
18. Calafati A.G. (2010), *Economie in cerca di città*, Donzelli, Roma.
19. Chiatti C., Orazi F. (2012), *Invecchiamento demografico e sviluppo ecosistemico urbano nelle città della Terza Italia*, in Calafati A.G. (ed.), *Le città della terza Italia. Evoluzione strutturale e sviluppo economico*, Franco Angeli Milano.
20. In literature, there are many definitions of social capital, often conflicting among them. However, among these, all share one element: reference to a relational dimension. Social capital always presents itself as a resource based on the existence of some kind of relationship, which gives life to a body of active interconnections between people: trust, confidence, mutual understanding and sharing of values and attitudes able to cement members of a network or community, thus making cooperative actions possible. Putnam R. (2000) *Bowling Alone. The Collapse and Revival of American Community*, New York, Touchstone–Simon & Schuster; Cohen D.J., Prusak L. (2001), *L*inking *Cooperation to the Economic Concept 'Capital' Signals*, Harvard Business School Press.
21. Bagnasco A. (1999), *Tracce di comunità*, Il Mulino, Bologna; Bagnasco A. (2001), Teoria del capitale sociale e «political economy» comparata, in Bagnasco A., Piselli F., Pizzorno A., Trigilia C. (eds.), *Il capitale sociale Istruzioni per l'uso*, Bologna Il Mulino, 2001; Paci M. (1999), Alle origini dell'imprenditorialità e della fiducia interpersonale nelle aree a economia diffusa, in Gruppo di Ancona (ed.), *Trasformazioni dell'economia e della società italiana*, Il Mulino, Bologna; Pizzorno A. (2001): Perché si paga il benzinaio. Per una teoria del capitale sociale, in Bagnasco A., Piselli F., Pizzorno A., Trigilia C. (eds.), *Il capitale sociale Istruzioni per l'uso*, Il Mulino, Bologna. Trigilia C. (2001), Capitale sociale e sviluppo locale, in Bagnasco A., Piselli F., Pizzorno A., Trigilia C., *Il capitale sociale. Istruzioni per l'uso*, Il Mulino, Bologna.

22. Trigilia C. (1986), *Grandi partiti e piccole imprese*, Il Mulino, Bologna.
23. Socci M. (2012), *Le classi dirigenti locali in Italia*, Cattedrale, Ancona.
24. Coleman J. (1990), *Foundations of Social Theory,* Harvard University Press, Cambridge, Mass.
25. Cartocci R. (2007), *Mappe del tesoro*, Il Mulino, Bologna.
26. Mutti A. (1998), *Capitale sociale e sviluppo*, Il Mulino, Bologna.
27. The relationships between social system and personality structure work in the same way as a complementarity relationship and allow the analysis of individual action in relation to codifications and norms that determine the social field of its possibilities. For example, addressing the problem of individual adaptation methods, Robert K. Merton made a distinction between conformity, innovation, ritualism, renunciation and rebellion, recognizing in the first the ability to guarantee stability and social continuity in terms of cultural goals and institutionalized means to pursue them (see Merton R.K. (1957), *Social Theory and Social Structure*, Free Press, Columbia University, New York). Gerth H., Wright Mills C. (1953), *Character and Social Structure*, Harcourt, Brace and Co., New York, elaborated a categorization centred on the variables of internal and external conformity to norms, in which we distinguish rigourists, conformists (opportunists), hypocrites and rebels. Riesman D., Glazer N., Denney R. (1950). *The Lonely Crowd: A Study of the Changing American Character,* Yale University Press, along the same line of investigation on the relationship between social system and personality structure, proposed a distinction between eras depending on whether the tradition-directed individual, the self-directed individual—essentially the puritan modern man—or the hetero-directed individual—essentially the romantic hedonist—prevails.
28. Steiner P. (2011), *La sociologie économique*, La Découverte & Syros, Paris.
29. Polanyi K. (1944). *The Great Transformation*, Farrar & Rinehart, New York.

30. Trigilia C. (1998), *Sociologia economica, stato, mercato e società nel capitalismo moderno*, Il Mulino, Bologna.
31. Sewell W.H. (2005), *Logics of History. Social Theory and Social Transformation*, by The University of Chicago.
32. For a discussion of the debate, see: Ben B., Ellen L. (1990), Consumerism and the Industrial Revolution, in *Social History* pp. 151-179; Braudel F. (1979), *Civiltà materiale, economia e capitalismo. Le strutture del quotidiano*, Einaudi, Torino; Capuzzo P. (2006), *Culture del consumo*, Il Mulino, Bologna; Cavazza S., Scarpellini E. (2006), *Il secolo dei consumi*, Carocci, Roma; De Grazia V. (2005), *Irresistible Empire. America's Advance Through Twentieth-Century Europe*, Cambridge (Mass.), Belknap Press; Glennie P. (1995), Consumption within Historical Studies, in Miller D. (ed.), *Ackowledging Consumption. A Review of News Sudies*, Routledge, London-New York; McCracken G.D. (1990), *Culture and Consumption: New Approaches to the Symbolic Character of Consumer Goods and Activities*, Indiana University Press; McKendrick N., Brewer J., Plumb J.H. (1982), *The Birth of a Consumer Society. The Commercialization of Eighteenth-Century England*, Bloomington, Indiana University Press; Mukherji C. (1983), *From Graven Images: Patterns of Modern Materialism*, Columbia University Press, New York; Sassatelli R. (1997), Consuming Ambivalence. Eighteenth-Century Public Discourse on Consumption and Mandeville's Legacy, in *Journal of Material Culture*, pp. 339-360; Sassatelli R. (2004), *Consumo, cultura e società*, Il Mulino, Bologna.
33. Giddens A. (1984), *The Constitution of Society: Outline of the Theory of Structuration*, Polity Press, Cambridge; Giddens A. (1990), *The Consequences of Modernity*, Stanford University Press.
34. Bagnasco A. (2016), *La questione del ceto medio. Un racconto del cambiamento sociale*, Il Mulino, Bologna.
35. Bourdieu P. (1979), La *Distinction. Critique sociale du jugement*, Minuit, Paris.
36. Durkheim É. (2003), *Les formes* élémentaires de la vie religieuse, Presses Universitaires de France; Searle J.R. (2010), *Making*

*the Social World. The Structure of Human Civilization*, Oxford University Press.

37. It is an open and debated problem in the social sciences whether the influence that the economic field exerts on social hierarchy, that is on the distribution and organization of social inequalities, is exclusive of the sphere of production relations or also contemplates those of consumption. Giddens, for example, in describing the process of structuring the social classes, that is, their formation as a dynamic that from market conflicts, where groups are differentiated by resources and interests, leads to their identification as structured social forms, considers among the sources proximate to structuring the influence exerted by distribution groups. According to Bagnasco (2016, p. 85), "With this opening, Giddens does not intend to distance himself from the idea that social classes are phenomena that involve production. However, he affirms that shared consumption patterns are particularly relevant for the concrete structuring of classes". Indeed, consumption methods can interact both with the sphere of working relationships, in which the social division of tasks structure social differences, defining homogeneous production processes, and with the systems of authority of organization aimed at clearly separating roles and functions in the productive process (executors, decision makers, overseers). This is possible sincepeople attribute meaning to reality, expressing it then through specific symbolic systems that are part of their culture. In other words, men create with their actions the meanings by which they are able to provide a sense to the social dimension of their own lives. Such a mechanism assumes a fundamental function in the maintenance and reproduction of the society in which they live. Veblen (1953); Dumazedier J. (1967), *Vers une civilisation du loisir*, ed. Du Seuil, Paris; Bourdieu (1979).
38. Castronovo V. (2010), *L'Italia del miracolo economico*, Laterza, Roma-Bari.
39. Pasolini P.P. (1975), *Scritti corsari. Gli interventi più discussi di un testimone provocatorio*, Garzanti, Milano.

40. Campbell, C. (1987), *The Romantic Ethic and the Spirit of Modern Consumerism*, Writersprintshop Press.
41. The social and cultural changes that arose from the Renaissance to the beginning of the twentieth century made man conscious of having greater power and greater autonomy of judgment with regard to reality. This allowed the affirmation of the "self-directed" individual (inner-directed man) (Riesman, 1950). Living in an tradition-shattering age, the self-directed type is aware of the existence of conflicting traditions and the need to adapt to changing social exigencies. The contrast between familiar habitus and public life is composed of the gyroscope mechanism whereby the person can receive certain signals from the outside and internalize them on condition that he can reconcile himself with the limited possibility of manoeuvring that the gyroscope allows. This reception takes place via communication channels (e.g. novels, poetry anthologies, newspapers, etc.) where the receiving reader controls, with a certain degree of autonomy, the semiotic relationship with the issuing author. The sensory structures immersed in reading-reception-processing, even if orientated by imaginary fantastic fabrics, do not provide for the absolutization of the sensorial and receptive relationship imposed by electronic media. Furthermore, registers and canons of communication still distinctly separate morality, ethics and aesthetics.
42. Campbell (1987) reconsidering the Weberian theses on the "spirit of capitalism", emphasizes the link between the industrial revolution and consumption patterns. The Protestant ethic of a Puritan matrix is only seemingly opposed to the advent of the logic of consumption. In reality, it is precisely its pietistic evolution that nourishes a new imaginative culture fundamental in achieving that romantic ethic on the ethical and moral basis of consumption cultures. The romantic ethic described by Campbell has fed an ideal of sentimentalism that has allowed the ego to valorise the themes of pleasure and projective and mimetic fantasy. This allows each individual symbolic identification with a multiplicity of aesthetic models whose source is fuelled by the growing access to consumption recorded in Europe as early as the

eighteenth century, which transformed a very large portion of the globe into a symbolic and material continuum of collective values and behaviour, of identifying statuses and of conformist models.

43. Pizzorno A. (1974), I ceti medi nel meccanismo del consenso, in Cavazzae L., Graubard S.R. (eds.), *Il caso italiano*, Garzanti, Milano.
44. Asquer E. (2011), *Storia intima dei ceti medi. Una capitale e una periferia nell'Italia del miracolo economico,* Laterza, Roma-Bari.
45. Redfield R., Linton R., Herskovits M.J., (1936), A Memorandum for the Study of Acculturation, American, Anthropologica, Association.

**Map of the Fourth Capitalism in Italy**

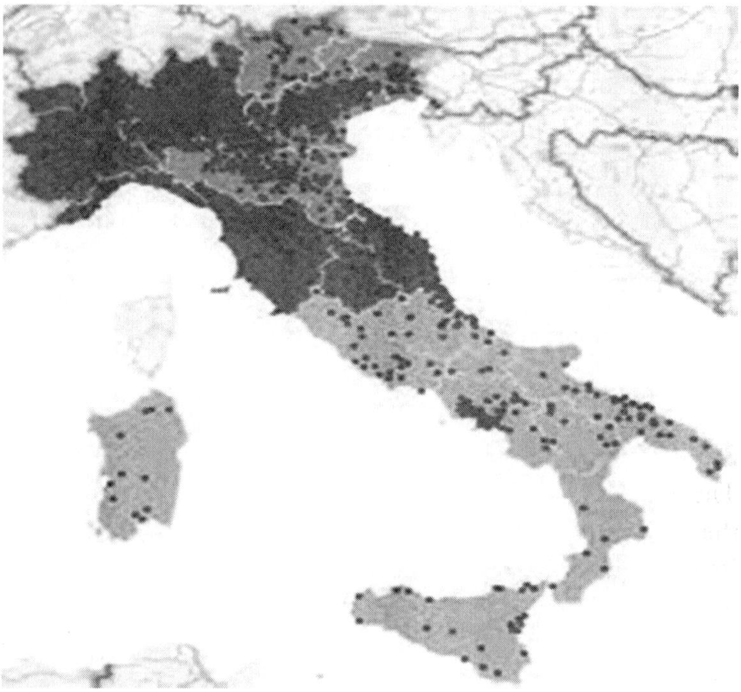

Source: Mediobanca-Unioncamere 2017.

The fourth capitalism consists of companies in the intermediate size segment, neither large nor small, generally distinguished by an international presence and partially attributable to local production systems. The map shows the territorial concentration gap, represented by the density of red spots, between Center-North and South plus Islands.

# 3

# Polycentrism and Institutions

## 3.1 The Geographically Small and Provincial

The growing power of local and regional authorities is one of the most fascinating phenomena of the "experiment" that is Italy in the past 30 years. It can be linked partially to the large-scale relaunch of local economic development, whose policies and institutions constitute an essential stimulus for promotion and consolidation.

Moreover, since the 1990s, the somewhat controversial federalist view proposed by Lega Nord[1] has advocated a newly important role for the geographically small, in symmetry and synergy with the European federalist approach which reflects the spirit of the age: geographical globalism.[2] At the turn of the twentieth century in particular, "Italian-style" federalism has led to significant changes in the relationship between the centre and the periphery, caused by a decentralization of power and institutional functions partly driven by the success of powerful local elites which include entrepreneurs in the *quarto capitalismo* sector, managers, journalists and leading professional figures. In the years preceding the recent economic crisis, there was an expectation that the local and regional ruling classes would be able to ensure effective local governance. On the contrary: a path-dependency interpretation highlights that the disappointing course our country has taken in recent years is actually due to the continuation of local centripetal forces which fragment the country-wide system, crushing it into local polycentrism and resulting in a system which is far from open.[3]

From Italian unification till the second half of the twentieth century, local and regional political elites were seen by Italian political literature as the expression of "grass-roots" politics, a kind of pseudo-elite bound to particular municipal contexts, local business interests and groups with limited prospects. For many years they were not considered as elites, as they lacked real autonomy. After all, the history of Italy's unification, initially as a monarchy and then the first twenty-five years as a republic, was characterized by the centralized approach of the country's institutions.[4]

As mentioned in Chapter 1, an undervaluation similar to that of the local institutions and elites also affected the development of the provinces during the 1970s and 80s, and the small and medium-size businesses involved in such development.[5] For decades these were seen as a problem rather than a resource for the country's production structure; difficult to organize and manage through centralist policies of industrialization and modernization. Political and economic localism, then, was long considered synonymous with backwardness, intimately linked with a provincial social and cultural closed-mindedness to influence and change from outside.[6]

The attitude towards the rich fabric of small and medium-size businesses underwent a partial shift during the 1980s. On the one hand, studies of the region known as the Third Italy and the economy of the regions demonstrated that the local development of SMEs in industrial districts scattered throughout the area was turning Italy into an industrial country on a European and global level: the Republic of Italy was experiencing a second genuine economic boom in the centre and north-east to follow the first, based on the principles of Fordism and Taylorism, which occurred in the north-west of the country during the 1950s and 60s.[7] So Italy suddenly appeared to be rich in terms of autonomous, open local development—from industrial districts to tourism and culture—able to offer a good level of social self-determination, fuel its own development from within and establish relations with international—and subsequently, global—markets.[8]

During the last quarter of the twentieth century, the benefits of the geographically small in terms of "provincial" development and well-being became apparent. In the meantime, the evident limitations of the national political elite—seen as incapable of carrying out its function as a ruling class—led some academics to reconsider the often innovative (and not obstructionist) role played by the political elite and by local economic and cultural classes in the modernization of Italy since before the country's unification.[9]

The shift towards regionalization in our institutional architecture which began in the 1970s was welcomed by some academics as a significant reversal in the movement towards decentralization.[10] This process, which by 2011 had resulted in 146,000 elected posts in the regions, provinces and local authorities, was set in motion by law 81 of 1993 to introduce the direct election of mayors and provincial presidents. This occurred following Tangentopoli and the deep crisis in particracy during the early days of the Republic, on the knife-edge of delegitimizing the central institutions after the defenestration of the political elite surrounding the CAF coalition of Craxi, Andreotti and Forlani.

The shift in public opinion that drove Tangentopoli created the illusion of a new era of grass-roots democratic participation that could engage interested citizens. The illusion appeared able to bring institutions together in a federal style, encouraging government by "proximity". However, the regional authorities did not fully grasp the opportunities presented by the constitutional reforms no.1 in 1999 and no.3 in 2001 (see Section V). The autonomy granted to regional and local institutions was unable to trigger development in a more complex and globalized context, particularly in the south of the country. Instead, we witnessed a relative decline of the entire country.[11]

Naturally, a distinction should be made between the performance of regional political elites, which are likely to be partially due to the legacy of past administrations: from the Habsburgs to the centralism of the Savoys, Austrians and Bourbons, and later the "red and white" subcultures. From 2001 to the present day, regional and local elites have nevertheless followed a course which replicates, on a smaller scale, the self-referential approach of the central elite, as evidenced by the default of the Sicily Region in summer 2012 and that of Lazio and Lombardy in winter of the same year. In these cases, entrenched particularism and neopatrimonialism in the exercise of local politics have effectively commandeered ideas and resources of general benefit.

Local and regional elites have similarly become the focus of media attention, their activities personalized, financed and professionalized. This metamorphosis describes local and regional elites trained by the "close ranks" (or foxes) of the various leaders (or lions) behind today's political parties, struck down by the collapse of their militants and reduced to voter-pleasing sound bites by political marketing.

## 3.2 The Polycentric Roots of Political Elites

For centuries, territorial polycentrism has tyrannized the Italian peninsula, linked with the centripetal force of localism which itself is driven by widespread urban development in thousands of communities all over the country (more than 8,000 comunes): the result is a thorough and diffuse nationwide local system and limited hegemony by major cities. Polycentrism[12] has had a marked impact on the culture of local administration and hence on the country's nation-building. This may actually be the cause of a widespread lack of a sense of state among citizens, which could be seen as passive resistance to centralist tendencies. Thanks to this stubborn resilience, polycentrism and localism have never lost their effective power, even during the most centralistic periods in Italy's history such as the early twentieth century, the Fascist era and the postwar reconstruction.[13]

Since the beginning of the Republic, the relationship between the centre and regions, distorted by Italy's polycentric structure, has passed through three phases. The first of these is the centralism of the postwar reconstruction years and the first economic boom. This period was guided by the fathers of the republican constitution and an elite dominated by moralisers; the Italian Communist Party itself, under Togliatti, supported centralism. The arrangement was top-down, from centre to periphery. This period saw the reorganization of the social order, starting with the concrete reconstruction of local communities. The country was united by the shared difficulties of national rebuilding; in fact differentiated conditions existed from the outset, with a lack of uniformity in the organization of societies and associations and administrative cultures that varied from one region to the next. The special status of the Autonomous Regions was established, but regionalism remained dormant under the Christian Democrat coalition of the DC. The second phase is centralism mitigated by the start of regionalization processes during the 1970s. This period saw Italy's political leadership moving into the hands of "negotiators" and the reemergence of the autonomous regions, now supported by socialist-communist local authorities, but also by association with the "white", Christian-Democrat subculture. The nature of the relationship between centre and periphery changes. In this period the great social pacts were established and the importance of the autonomous regions was once again acknowledged by a national elite of negotiators. However, only a few regional political classes, such as those of Emilia Romagna and Tuscany, benefited from this "breaking-in" period.[14] During these years, an underground competition was being fought; a "camouflage" war between red and white subcultures. The red subculture prevailing in certain crucial regions opposed the central government of the DC party. Similarly, the white subculture occupied the central government uninterruptedly for the first two-thirds of Italy's current republican period. The regional red subculture, repositioned in a large middle-class swathe of Italians, stimulated the aggregating effect of the local body, adopting continuous concertation and networking of services as central strategies. For the white subculture, the paradigms of social action have always been Catholic associationism and market forces; a problematic combination with varying emphasis among the political elite of Lombardy and the Veneto, but in both cases focused on the market and individual consumer choice. The passive attitude of many regional political classes in the constitutional phase of the 1970s—particularly widespread in the southern regions—nevertheless displayed an ability to contradict and resist policies adopted by central government, instigating well-oiled mechanisms of patronage welfare systems and turning the traditional notability into professional politicians surrounded by local cliques. In many of the nascent regional bodies nepotism abounded; the public sector became a place where profits could be made without the need to deliver services. Indeed, services were implemented according to employment and supplementary income. The regional councillor and the mayor also became the employers of their clients.

## 3.3 Federalist Decentralization and Multi-level Government

The third phase in the relationship between centre and periphery is characterized by federalist decentralization and multi-level government, which reached its apex during the two "Berlusconi decades" under the federalist flag, cutting across both right and left of the political spectrum. Italy's post-Tangentopoli political elites, consisting increasingly of "persuaders", made a virtue of necessity by giving rein to federalist reform which would actually result in a considerable increase in the number, remuneration and privileges of elected and appointed positions at the local and regional level. The centre-periphery relationship was complicated by the highly intrusive power of globalization, and the polycentric force reemerged.

With the new century, regional political classes gained new importance as an intermediate centre of gravity between centre and periphery, despite the fact that there is a common tendency to favour vertical subsidiarity over administrative levels lower in the hierarchy. With this shared approach, the regional political classes then diversified: while in Emilia and Veneto the elite and the culture appear to be polycentric, with high and low levels of horizontal institutions. For example, Tuscany and Lombardy—although each with their differences—moved more towards dirigisme.

There is no doubt that in the course of the Second Republic, considerable internal transformations have occurred within the white and red areas, which have impacted voting habits. In the white north-east, the Lega has taken the baton from the DC, turning the region from white to green. In "middle Italy", on the one hand a major redefinition is ongoing of the balances and relationships of internal power, particularly between Emilia-Romagna and Tuscany; with the consolidation of this bi-polar arrangement, the latter exerts a centre-left political and electoral hegemony which has long been the preserve of the former. On the other hand, both red and white areas are seeing the growth of abstentionism and the advancement of new political entities such as M5S. Between 2005 and 2010, the red regions saw a considerable drop in turnout (down 9.1 per cent on average), more than the national average drop of 8 per cent. Disenchantment and abstentionism in these regions appear to cast doubt on the accepted Putnam-style interpretation based on the idea of central Italy as a participatory and virtuous electorate characterised by widespread networks of loyalty and civic spirit and able to prioritise high levels of value in local government. In the red areas, the Democratic Party (PD) remains dominant, but its base is being eroded to the point that it is losing the "centrality" which saw the PCI (Communist Party) as the focus of local institutions and associations.

Southern Italy is a case apart, since weak centralism has led to a new local professional ruling class which is centred on consensus management and thus lowers the quality of politics, administration and community.[15] Nevertheless, even the leaders and elites of certain southern cities and regions have attempted to bring change and innovation to the southern administrative culture, for example Antonio Bassolino's first term in Naples and the "Spring of the Mayors", the case of Basilicata or, more recently, with mayor of Naples Luigi De Magistris. These are not so much false starts as somewhat unsuccessful attempts, precisely because of the *gattopardismo* of local interest groups, who deploy their mimetic power to ride the wave of innovation and change. The truth is that political elites in the north are also conditioned by clientelism and patronage, although here the apparatus of government, society and the market are more solid. In northern public administration, links between politics and business have expanded with greater autonomy, and are often exposed to Mafia and Camorra.

Between 2001 and 2014, local and regional elites were seen first and foremost as a way out of the problems of national political representation; after 2006, they fell into corruption and intense criticism of the political caste. So what happened? The growth of autonomous local and regional power has allowed the political elites of the regions to assimilate the vices of the national elite. In terms of resources made available on the political market, they are primarily concerned with local redistribution (lobby groups). In this way, they create a kind of local neo-corporatism in which the political class, by consensus government, appears increasingly determined to reproduce itself, without prioritizing strategies necessary for the social and economic development of their regions.

The (apolitical?) discontent of citizens becomes evident, for example, in the local elections of 2012, in which record numbers of abstentions were registered (particularly in Sicily), and also the 2013 elections (including Basilicata) with a collapse in consensus particularly towards the parties holding the power in local and regional administrations. In the 2014 regional elections in Emilia Romagna, abstentions exceeded 62 per cent. The reputation of local and regional elites has plummeted in the eyes of a population anxious about their vast cost, the waste in the vast and Byzantine multi-level institutional architecture and the inadequate performance of our country's decentralised governing bodies. Furthermore, the lack of democracy within parties, poor levels of transparency in their conduct, the concentration of power in the hands of limited groups and the frequent scandals affecting various politicians have fuelled numerous campaigns of popular protest—led by Grillo's M5S and Salvini's Lega.[16]

The national political elite have responded to the waves of protest with plans for institutional reform, which to date remain vague promises. However, they have taken advantage of growing dissatisfaction with regional and local elites to impose heavy cuts in the allocation of state resources to the regions. The effect of such austerity measures is to create concrete problems in the provision of services to citizens, further damaging the reputation and trust in local and regional political elites.

As we will see in the coming chapters, there is no connection between the degree of well-being in an area and the remuneration of its local political class, and local and regional administrations find themselves with high levels of debt. At least four regions (Calabria, Sicily, Lazio and Campania) are in serious trouble owing to clear violations of their statutes and the constitution: this situation amounts to a real "failure of the autonomous regions", despite the fact that these regions handle budgets of approximately 220 billion euros. Weak or non-existent checks by central government, consociational practices that use spending as leverage and exorbitant policy costs linked to increasing autonomy in local and regional bodies translate to an arbitrary latitude among the regional political classes, giving rise to a series of serious distortions in regional accounts.

This critical state of institutional performance is concentrated in the southern regions, although problems of overall debt and healthcare funding are also found in central and northern regions (Lazio, Piemonte and Valle d'Aosta). Many local and regional governments therefore find themselves in circumstances of inadequate performance and highly vulnerable to clientelism and criminal infiltration, issues which will be addressed in greater detail in the next chapter. In such cases, the consequences are a two-level society and welfare system (such as the disparity between north and south, for example). The recent reductions in resources allocated by central government to the regions and local bodies have increased the differences in the provision of welfare services, since only the administrations of regions with a higher GDP are able to make up for the cuts with their own resources and ensure adequate levels of service provision.

## 3.4 Chaotic Polycentrism

Areas divided by levels of economic development, fragmentation in the provision of welfare services, differences in overall debt and healthcare services in debit, and the high costs of the political and bureaucratic apparatus call into question the actions and responsibilities of local and—particularly—regional political elites. As a whole, these appear to be ageing, exclusively male preserves, bound by loyalty to the bosses of their parties. However, their social composition is undergoing profound change, partly due to the growing attractiveness of the main local jobs. In some cases a local and regional post may be preferable to a parliamentary one. Not to mention the power of the mayors of large cities or the regional presidents, referred to as governors and treated on a par with the princes of the regional states Italy once comprised—like an institutional mosaic—in the Middle Ages and prior to unification. The attraction of certain top seats in major cities and important regions, as we have seen, has reshaped the course of political careers, breaking the one-way route from periphery to centre: hence the growing importance of local and regional political leaders with a national profile.[17]

Research demonstrates that with the disappearance of the mass parties, the post-Tangentopoli political class was weakened to the point where it needed reinforcements, and suffered incursions from other professions, the most important being entrepreneurs, managers and journalists, evidence of the increasing financialization and mediatization of politics. However, research also indicates that, following the period of reshuffling of local politicians that occurred in the early 1990s as a result of the institutional crisis and particracy, Italy saw a "backwash" of civic society among elected politicians, with a resurgence of the ruling class closely related to professional politics, which once again occupied top posts in local and regional government. Like Lampedusa's Gattopardo, this new ruling class was able to ride the wave of reform and innovation introduced during the federalist period, while retaining intact its mechanisms of patronage. Here again is a constant and long-standing feature: the multiple stances of the political big-shots.

There is growing emphasis on personality, and professionals with greater resources in terms of connections, reputation and personal prestige marketable on the local political scene are at an advantage. Conversely, there is a decline in the popular aspect (workers, artisans etc) in terms of their representation in local politics, which was once dependent on parties of the masses. This component has become practically invisible, even more so than young people after their incursion into the control room with M5S MPs. While Italy's republican past perhaps shows the contribution of local politics to the development of the country as a whole, today—after twenty years of gradual shift of the centre of gravity from the centre to the periphery (over 60 per cent of the country's public spending has been decentralised)—it is clear that the drive towards federalism, which began with the electoral and constitutional reforms at the turn of the millennium, is breaking apart on the rocks of the chaotic polycentrism of Italy's "reformed" politics. The result is a patchwork of territories administered differently in terms of the culture and performance of local government.

It would therefore be apt to speak of a lost opportunity for the local—and particularly regional—political classes, which are seen as an important focal point for multi-level government; a missed opportunity and expectations evaporated, since the newly personal and presidential style of local electioneering of the early 1990s had legitimized regional and provincial presidents and mayors from the new ruling class in "proximity politics".

The missed opportunity and the evaporation of expectations are confirmed, for example, by the fact that the trustworthiness of local and regional authorities is rated by Italians at an average of 3.9, barely higher than trust in Parliament (3.7, with parties at 2.5). This is a serious lack of trust, underlined by the fact that our country is among the lowest-ranking in Europe in terms of trust in local authorities. Faced with the economic crisis and the harsh criticism of politics and its double inefficiency (in public administration), the functioning of local and regional governments is seen by citizens in more or less the same way as national government: unable to provide solutions to the serious problems afflicting the country. Whereas till 2005 the progress (albeit uncertain and wobbly) of federalism appeared to offer an increasingly bright future for regional and local politics to the detriment of the national elite, in the second decade of this century, many observers believe that the regional and local political class may be entering a new period of decline, a kind of downgrading or marginalization, because of the limits of the elite itself. This view is encouraged by a national political class who in the absence of strategic ideas and decisions, have proceeded with across-the-board cuts without any clear strategy for sectors or systems. However, the quantitative increase in local elites has resulted in serious backwardness in vision and in the ability to handle social, economic and political transformation on the global scale.[18]

First and foremost Brussels is regarded as far more important than Rome; politics has extended its field of action and its "market" at local and regional level and strengthened as a local political force, but only rarely has it aroused interest among citizens and involved them in high-quality politics geared to the benefit of all. In fact this has hardly ever happened, given the low levels of trust earned by local political elites.

Secondly, this lack of trust has gained reception thanks to the inadequate performance of local and regional political classes. In other words, politicians do not take enough notice of the underlying problems which link local issues to national, European and global issues. Instead, local politicians are occupied with the demands of the short-term nature of the electoral cycle and the consequent need for short to medium-term projects whose results are visible and valuable as a marketing tool in the gaining of consensus in the local arena (permanent election campaign). In the best of cases the outcome is a performative pragmatism which is necessary, but not sufficient to boost the region's competitiveness and quality.

Thirdly, local political classes have picked up from their central elders a tendency to self-referentiality. These are politicians who, for example, have extended their scope with small-scale laws to establish minor new provinces, increase the number of councillors and raise salaries and benefits. The supply of representation has increased despite the fact that approximately half of Italians believe elected posts should be reduced and provincial authorities abolished. It is therefore a supply that tends to exceed demand, which in fact seeks transparency, simplicity, effectiveness, linearity and a certain amount of boldness in order to innovate and lead a local area.

## 3.5 Institutional Performance and the Governance of Socio-Economic Development

Italian political culture and its institutions are characterised by a troubled relationship between centre and periphery, which has impacted negatively on the performance of local governments and failed to resolve the socio-economic imbalances of the Italian regions. The issue of institutional performance concerns the improvement of administration and is often an indicator of innovative governance in which the decision-making mechanisms of local government are supported by social participation and the use of technology (institutional entrepreneurship). In this way a positive correlation is established between social involvement, technology and administrative efficiency. The outcome is that the working of democracy and the functions of government are far more efficient, particularly when dealing with an active community based on relationships of trust, reciprocity and networks of civic responsibility. The institutional entrepreneur must interpret contexts and encourage their valorisation, particularly in the global competition between regions, employing private-sector tools for assessment, management and checking while retaining the "public value" of initiatives. However, the Italian model of institutional performance and its impact on economic development remains stuck in a (structuralist) vision in which the long history of the accumulation of social capital and its effects on path dependence have the effect of neutralising political action based on economic circumstances, thus reducing social, economic and technological innovation to epiphenomena. Conversely, the following pages highlight the extent to which government efficiency impacts the dynamics of local development, as well as the need for a renewed role for public actors to guide local economies towards institutional and socio-economic modernisation. Especially in the southern regions of Italy, which lack the resources to escape the trap of low productivity, the public sector needs to implement targeted measures and take on a role of guidance for development. This aim has often failed, at least when we consider the experiences of programmes carried out in Italy in recent decades.[19]

## 3.6 Immobility and Decline: The Past and Present of a Country Split Between North and South

Italy today is one of the EU countries with the greatest inequality in wealth distribution: In 2017, relative poverty it involved 3 million 171 thousand households (12.3 per cent, against 10.6 per cent in 2016), and 9 million 368 thousand individuals (15.6 per cent compared to 14.0 per cent the previous year); the percentage of the population on low incomes is 45 per cent in Sicily and 37 per cent in Campania and Calabria, compared with 6 per cent in the north of the country.[20]

Inequality also affects access to healthcare in the central and northern regions compared to the south. A recent report by Census estimates that in 2018, 7 million Italians fell into debt to pay for private healthcare.[21] Despite a universal national health system, in 2017, Italians spent 40 billion euros on private treatment. Here there are sharp discrepancies between north and south, with the latter suffering from unmanageable waiting lists and structural disorganisation in the provision of services. In other words, more people are dying in the south than in the centre and north Italy, and life expectancy is falling, with Campania at the very bottom of the list.[22] Political mismanagement and low healthcare spending affect the provision of treatment and prevention, and therefore outcomes for individuals.

In parallel with this situation, economic inequality and the concentration of wealth is growing, both in terms of hard figures and in the perception of the population, especially in southern Italy. The socio-economic equity index rises from 141 to 143 for the north-east, but falls from 72 to 71 for the south. The north-west drops three points from 142 to 139, and the centre from 123 to 120. Trentino (167), Lombardy (152) and Emilia Romagna (148) lead the classification of the most successful regions. These figures highlight the link between the growth of hardship and the growth of inequality. The general index of quality of development fell from 100 to 99 between 2015 and 2016, with a worsening in particular in the centre and north of the country.[23] But what really concerns the south is that there is no reduction of the long-standing gap between it and the rest of the country. The best-performing regions overall are Trentino Alto Adige (136), Friuli Venezia Giulia (113) and Veneto (112), while Campania, Sicily and Calabria are at the bottom of the table. This gap relates both to income per capita—a well-known fact—and to inequality in the distribution of income and wealth. And it is no accident: the larger regions of southern Italy suffer from the destructive effect of Mafia activity. This makes businesses afraid to embark on risky activities, contaminates the transparency of public administration, undermines the culture of lawfulness and causes a lack of trust and social cohesion as well as considerable economic distortion. An example of such damaging circumstances can be found in a comparison with East Germany after the country's reunification. In 1991, southern Italy was in a better economic situation than East Germany. By 1993, however, the eastern states of Germany had overtaken southern Italy in terms of both GDP per capita and employment. In 1991 East Germany's GDP per capita was just over 30 per cent of the figure in the West of the country; two years later it exceeded 60 per cent, rising to 70 per cent in recent years. In southern Italy, meanwhile, the same performance index actually remained immobile at just over 50 per cent of the per capita GDP of the north. What made the difference to the recovery of the eastern German states were the enormous transfers of public funds, both national and European (approximately 2,000 billion euros between 1991 and 2011). The same did not occur with the national and EC funding allocated to southern Italy: some 230 billion euros by 1993, and almost double that to date.[24] The difference in the performance of the public sector is affected by the combination of economic and political mismanagement due to Mafia criminality and the resulting poor quality in the functioning of local government and the ruling classes. This led to a situation in which the paradox of fickle resistance to political change (as in *Il Gattopardo*) meets the long-standing weakness of the Italian bourgeoisie (Gramsci) which, in the south of the country, is not only more acute, but coupled with a society fragmented into social groups with little moral density.[25] A deadly mix which undermines the foundations of any unifying structure for systemic cooperation between the various components of society.[26]

Moving to another hot topic—national insurance and pensions—there are clear regional differences in performance which will be difficult to sustain in the future.[27] If we examine contributions to INPS (the Italian national social security institute), for example, of the 134.823 billion euros received in 2015, 63.54 per cent came from the 8 northern Italian regions, 20 per cent from the 4 central regions and 16.44 per cent from the 8 southern regions. The same institute allocated a total of 176.947 billion, with the north receiving 55.86 per cent of the total, the centre 19.74 per cent and the south receiving 24.40 per cent, almost twice as much as it paid in. Every citizen in northern Italy contributes 3,086 euros, compared with 2,236 in the centre and just 1,008 in the south. If we calculate the per capita payments in relation to population, in pensions alone, the Italian state allocates every inhabitant of southern Italy more than 1,000 euros a year, against 658 in the central regions and 474 in the north. If on top of social security contributions we calculate direct taxes in the regional balance, along with all welfare spending (pensions, benefits, sickness and healthcare) the figures emerging indicate that the north of Italy produces a total of 27.18 billion euros and the centre 3.75 billion, while the south has a deficit of 36.36 billion, i.e. the entire output of the north and the centre plus approximately 6 billion euros. An examination of the detail of public spending by geographical area allows an evaluation to be made of the dynamics of the flow of incoming and outgoing funds in public finance. This allows us to identify the regions which are net beneficiaries and net contributors in the redistribution of funds which, we should remember, is not explicitly intended to rebalance regional inequalities. Redistribution is actually a normal activity for the public sector which provides services to all, financed by tax revenues predominantly raised according to a progressive tax rate structure. Overall, the surplus from the north and centre of the country finances the deficit in the south. This financial pattern reflects the higher tax-paying capacity of residents of the central and northern regions (who generally have higher incomes) given per capita spending levels which are relatively more uniform in all areas of the country. In the two-year period 2013-15, the south of Italy benefited from redistributed funding amounting to 4.2 per cent of GDP (18.7 per cent of GDP of the southern regions); since 2013 this sum has increased to recover most of the drop experienced in 2011-2012 in connection with the stability measures to consolidate public finances nationally. The total net contribution from the centre and north of the country amounted to 6.7 per cent of national GDP (8.6 per cent of regional GDP).[28] This situation results in a country which is "immobile" but structurally in precarious balance, in which the south still produces almost half the entire national debt and the north, thanks to multiple factors—the single currency, the ageing population, increased welfare provision and the economic crisis—is reducing its share of the surplus. The effect of this tendency is felt in the competitiveness of the Italian regions within the EU. Lombardy—as in the past—continues to be Italy's most competitive region, but this is in the overall context of the national economy and the performance of the regions, whose competitiveness deteriorated in almost every case between 2010 and 2016. The exceptions are Basilicata, Molise, Umbria and Marche, whose positions have remained unchanged since 2013, while Trentino Alto Adige and Aosta have improved.[29] If all the regions were at least 75 per cent self-sufficient, there would be no deficit and more than one percent of GDP could be invested in public infrastructure, assets and resources, which have been needed for too long in many areas. Even with such clear evidence this remains an insurmountable obstacle and the cause of institutional failures which over time have become chronic and which typify the Italian paradox and the internal polarization of its economy, society and politics.

To understand Italy is to accept its plurality. There are at least three different Italys. One historically established in the north-west, one more recently developed in the centre and based on small and medium-sized businesses organized in districts, and one in the south in which neither large public-sector firms nor the dynamics of internal local development have permitted adequate growth in terms of socio-economic density.

Whether the analysis is in terms of social capital (lack of trust networks) or in terms of structural economic differentiation (under-capitalization of the economy and peripherality/dependence of production systems), the south's failure to thrive is also the failure of an endogenous ruling class which is historically inefficient/ineffective and a fragile society with insufficient moral density relative to the collective interest (amoral familism and localism, clientelism and connivance with organized crime).

## 3.7 Political Autonomy without Economic Development: The Eclipse of Decentralization

The administrative and political decentralisation which began in the 1970s with the establishment of the regions and reached its idealogical conclusion with the reform of Title V of the Italian constitution in 2001[30] was the reflection of a claim to political autonomy both for regions capable of economic development (the industrialized fabric of 'Third Italy' and the Adriatic Corridor) and for regions which, due to the lack of political autonomy among their ruling classes, had not achieved sufficient levels in terms of economic performance and social development (the southern regions).[31] The direct election of city mayors and regional governments also concluded the period of administrative decentralization in relation to the political responsibility of elected figures, whose appointments are now increasingly bound by a more immediate relationship with the interests and needs of their areas and of local communities, voters, socio-economic bodies and peripheral lobby groups. The idea of development without autonomy, which had driven the political period of decentralization, has failed on many levels (see preceding paragraphs). Local political institutions have been highly inconsistent from region to region in their provision of improved management of resources and better services to citizens. In many cases political direction, governance of development and the performance of institutions have been undermined by the self-referentiality of the regional political classes and the local interests which bind them. This stranglehold has not been converted into a truly competitive relationship between the institutions of centre and periphery; on the contrary, it has led to an arrangement of reciprocal remuneration consisting of segments of votes needed by the centre and political careers which start in the provinces and extend towards Rome. An artificial emblem of this muddled situation is the idea that a good national leader is first and foremost a "Mayor for Italy", a rhetorical analogy often used as a supporting weapon in the growing disconnect between politicians and citizens.[32]

The aim of this chapter is to give a snapshot of the quality of the (institutional) performance obtained during Italy's period of administrative decentralization, assessing as far as possible its impact on the public finances of the country as a whole. So let us attempt to pick out a few figures to outline a framework for the questions we are addressing. Imbalances in performance between regional economies and governments, management discrepancies among politicians and a creeping mistrust of politics are traits that have characterized the relationship between institutions and citizens in the Italian regions in recent years.[33] One fact is emblematic as a summary of this deadlocked situation: in regions with the highest unemployment and the lowest per capita GDP, the remuneration of the governing individuals is higher than the average. This is an indicator of the inadequate institutional performance of local government, particularly in the southern regions of the country. In the case of Italy, however, there is more than this negative paradox in which the worst performers tend to be the best paid. The region of Emilia-Romagna is actually an interesting case study: a region which in many ways is virtuous, competitive and historically well-run.[34]

Albeit in the context of the generalized decrease in competitiveness of the Italian regions that occurred between 2010 and 2016 (Index of the Competitiveness of European Regions 2010, 2013, 2016), Emilia-Romagna is one of the driving forces of "Sistema Italia"; one of the regions that reacted most positively to crisis and worked the hardest to keep its economy in line with the European platform of development. At the same time it is the region with the best performance in terms of the ratio between governors' remuneration and per capita GDP

(Socci, 2012), and—as indicated in Table 1, it is the third Italian region in terms of the relationship between per capita public spending and GDP.[35]

**Table 1**

**Consolidated Public Spending in Italian Regions (Public Expenditure in per cent of GDP)**

| | |
|---|---|
| Calabria | 66,15% |
| Sardegna | 59,90% |
| Sicilia | 56,55% |
| Puglia | 54,80% |
| Molise | 54,69% |
| Basilicata | 54,03% |
| Campania | 52,96% |
| Friuli Venezia Giulia | 46,21% |
| Abruzzo | 45,74% |
| Umbria | 45,32% |
| Valle d'Aosta | 42,99% |
| Lazio | 42,51% |
| Liguria | 40,14% |
| Marche | 38,70% |
| Trentino Alto Adige | 35,82% |
| Piemonte | 35,60% |
| Toscana | 34,50% |
| Emilia Romagna | 30,28% |
| Veneto | 29,09% |
| Lombardia | 24,44% |

Source: Impresa Lavoro elaboration on data of the General Accounting of the State (2016).

Nevertheless, this is the region which experienced the greatest shock in terms of abstentionism, when its current regional government was elected in 2014 with the participation of just 37.71 per cent of voters. This apparent paradox is a litmus test for a country like Italy which is undergoing a profound change of political culture, and implicitly calls into question established paradigms of social science. For example, the question of social capital and its "structural" impact on local economies and institutions. Emilia Romagna, the emblematic region of Putnam's view of Italian civic culture, appears to have suddenly lost both the historic track of its positive path dependency, and the strength of its fabric of civic participation, a fundamental for the outcome of successful government. This is a shift which has deepened in the last quarter of a century and which highlights the extent to which politics—for good or for evil—conditions the structural factors of social and economic development. As occurred in Emilia Romagna after the Second World War, politics can generate a widespread and stimulating culture of participation, implement modern forms of local welfare and encourage industrialization and governance of local development which is highly competitive on the world stage. At the same time, if excessively smug and self-referential, politics can misplace the old game rules which govern the public interest. It can become an "iron cage"; not of subjugation, as Weber described bureaucracy, but of indolence. Politicians have lost their way; they seem to place too much trust in the path dependence that would like to see them unable to make too many mistakes, to truly account for the fate of their citizens, businesses and institutions. Politicians who are sheltered from the risk that their efforts and their merit might make a difference turn into an irresponsible elite, strengthened by the fact that no one is now required to set a good example and the exercise of power no longer needs authority, but pure procedure.[36] This is what happens in a society which has taken up the "burden" of virtues.[37] It should therefore not come as too much of a surprise that, even in local economies and socio-political communities which appear to be virtuous, the effective tearing of the link between public and private spheres should engender a "vendetta" among citizens with resounding exit strategies; just as when a product is boycotted by consumers due to the lack of credibility of the firm that makes it. Hence, although we are limited to a consideration of the potentially destructive impact politics may have on trust, we cannot help but count it as one of the human activities most closely connected with the sudden and often unexpected changes that the long course of history continues to present us with. In other words, the disconnect between collective perception and "objective statistics" is evidence of the progressive laceration occurring in Italy between political circles and civic society. The same thing appears to be evident today in the comparison—more symbolic than material—between the populace and the elite. Although this is a fiction created by the situation of permanent election campaign, this contrast brings concrete risk of slippage in an unstable terrain which no one—since the landslide of Tangentopoli—has ever addressed in the radical terms of a cultural and moral renewal of the country's ruling classes.

This general collective irresponsibility in our country on the part of its elites and ruling classes, and simultaneously its citizens, who over time have become more cynical players than responsible social actors, is expressed in a number of figures[38].

The regional balance sheets examined by the local sections of the Italian Court of Audit (2016) on the basis of 2015 financial statements reveal a total deficit by the Italian regions amounting to 33 billion euros, due primarily to the burden of debt associated with healthcare spending. This constitutes a weighty mortgage on the future possibility of many regions to implement policies to support welfare services and businesses, both of which are essential in order to revitalise the shaky growth of the Italian economy.

Moreover, Italian local governments are in a worrying level of debt, due to loans taken out with credit institutions. In 2017 the debts of autonomous provinces and regions amounted to 14 billion 780 million euros, compared with 14 billion the previous year. If the truth be told, considering their performance since the crisis began in 2008, debt to credit agencies has shown uneven dynamics. Although it has been increasing since the start of the crisis (14,649 billion euros), reaching its highest point in 2012 (17,438 billion), it then began to fall in 2013 and reached its lowest level since 2007 in 2016 (14,035 billion) Italian General Accounting of the State (2017). The regions' use of credit to access finance is influenced by two factors. The first, conjunctural aspect is the lower cost of money, which incentivises the recourse to borrowing; the second, structural aspect is the necessity of covering financial demands, when these are not sufficiently resourced by funds from central government. Between 2001 (4,062 billion euros) and 2017 (14,780 billion), residual debt to the credit system by autonomous regions and provinces varied by (...) per cent, indicating an increase in borrowing from private sector financial institutes by local administrations. Per capita public spending by individual Italian regions also shows a wide gap between virtuous regions and spendthrifts. An examination of the average over the three available years (2012 to 2014) shows a vast discrepancy between the 8,647 euros per capita per year spent in Lombardy and the 15,000 spent in the Aosta Valley or the 13,000-plus spent in Lazio.[39]

The regional difference in quantities spent is not a function of their geographical location: the north spends as much as the south. The difference lies in the quality of the spending. If we consider healthcare, for instance, the service provided in Lombardy is immeasurably better that that in Calabria, while the cost per capita is actually similar in both regions. This example highlights the need for improved monitoring of spending and greater control of political responsibility in the dynamics of local public finances. Improved services and less waste mean greater expertise in public administration and more political transparency. From public transport to the management and distribution of energy, all too often our public services are far from the optimal standards to be expected from their costs. This inefficiency is influenced by an excess of political intermediaries.

It is no longer sustainable that the Naples area—perhaps the region with the worst services for waste collection and disposal—should pay one of the highest tax rates in Italy. Neither are the costs of politics the same for everyone. The more than 42 euros per capita for the functioning of institutional bodies in Sardinia and the almost 32 euros for the same in Sicily contrast sharply with Piemonte and Emilia Romagna, where the cost is approximately 5 euros per year.

In Italy, the transfer of funds for current expenditure to public administration amounts to approximately 236 billion euros, almost half of the country's total expenditure (which in 2014 was a final balance of 504 billion, including 81 billion of interest both on national debt and budget deficit by public bodies).[40]

By evaluating the weight of public debt against this overall sum, we can calculate which regions are responsible for its growth, which in 2014 amounted to 47 billion euros.[41] From the figures it emerges that the driving force of Italian development, Lombardy, is the main generator of public debt with its 15 billion euros, followed by Lazio with 9.5 billion, Piemonte and Emilia Romagna with 4 billion, Veneto with 2.7 billion and Friuli Venezia Giulia with 2.5 billion. Regions like Sardinia and Basilicata have an extremely modest impact in percentage terms: together they produce 490 million of the increase in public debt, while Campania's contribution is considerable, at 2 billion euros.

Despite this hardly reassuring picture, the Italian regions have taken major steps towards improving their institutional performance, particularly in reducing the deficit in healthcare spending. The recent years of austerity have enabled the reduction of both the gaping deficits and the holes in local administration funding. In 2006 the shortfall between the allocation of public funds and actual spending amounted to 6 billion euros, which gradually fell to 1 billion 13 million in 2016, albeit slightly up from 928 million in 2014. The advantage of this was to allow the rebalancing of accounts in some regions: in 2006 Lazio alone had a deficit of 1 billion 966 million, almost double the national total for 2016; Sicily's deficit was over a billion, and Campania's was 750 million.

The programmes of debt repayment and restructuring initiated in 2007 involved Liguria, Lazio, Abruzzo, Molise, Campania, Sicily, Calabria and Sardinia. In Lazio, by 2016 the shortfall was down 164 million euros from the 2006 total of 1,966; Campania moved from -750 to +6.2 (but rose to +127 in 2014) and Sicily went from -1,088 million to a surplus of 700,000 euros.

Within this positive scenario there are exceptions, which in 2016 were the two worst-performing regions in terms of healthcare deficits: the autonomous province of Bolzano, which during these years never effectively reduced its deficit—227.8 million—and Sardinia, whose deficit increased from 129.2 million to 320.8. In 2016, the regions with the most positive accounts were Marche, with a surplus of 14.4 million, Piemonte with a surplus of 7.2 million, Campania with 6.2 and Umbria with 5.5.

However, the problem is not so much spending, but its quality. The table below illustrates the institutional performance of the Italian regions in terms of the relationship between taxation and services provided. Four clusters emerge. In the first—the virtuous regions—we find the administrations which have reduced taxes and improved levels of services (Abruzzo, Umbria, Marche) by a combination of restructuring spending and providing additional services. These are three regions which, in their different ways and with their different histories, constitute a semi-marginal piece of the corridor of Adriatic development which is unique in the history of reunited Italy and has transformed and expanded its production capacity, wealth and economic and social fabric. In the second group we find the regions that have decreased both taxes and services (insert regions). These are primarily regions in the south of Italy which have been forced—as we have just seen—to reduce their deficits, but which have been unable to translate this opportunity for debt restructuring into innovation and new service provision. The third cluster includes all the large central and northern regions (insert regions) which have increased taxation and services in parallel. Finally, in the fourth cluster—the negligent—we find Lazio, which although it has drastically reduced its healthcare deficit in the past decade, is the only Italian region to increase taxes while reducing services.

The issues discussed and the numerous paradoxes revealed in the performance of institutions offer plausible reasons as to why Italian democracy is today dominated by populist shortcuts, mediocratic technocracies and permanent electoral campaigns, in which pseudo truths render the credible useless, and cut through the troubled dream of a nation bewildered, ageing and tense.

## REFERENCES

1. The Northern League has been a party with a strong territorial and federalist connotation and in some historical moments also secessionist. The League ruled in Italy allying with the centre-right of Silvio Berlusconi. Today, after some vicissitudes including judiciary, the party is called Lega and the new leadership is characterized by a populist politics and a so-called sovereign programme. The League is in the coalition government with the Five Star Movement. The current political polls place it as the first party in Italy.
2. In this chapter, we will deal with political elites in their local dimension, on which we have an analysis within the Eliteam group, see Socci M. (2012), *Le classi dirigenti locali in Italia. Ceto politico ed élite economiche ai tempi della crisi*, Cattedrale, Ancona and Carboni C. (2015), Élite e ceto politico regionale, in Salvati M., Sciolla L. (eds.), *L'Italia e le sue regioni*, Treccani, Roma.
3. Carboni C. (2009), (ed.), *La governance dello sviluppo locale*, Il Mulino, Bologna.

4. In contrast, Anglo-American elitist literature (Wright Mills C., *The Power Elite*, Oxford University Press, New York, 1956; Hunter F., *Community Power Structure, A Study of Decision Makers*, University of North Carolina, Chapel Hill, 1953) and the pluralist (Dahl R., *Who Governs ?, Democracy and Power in an American City*, Yale University Press, New Haven, 1961), even though they have opposed sides, have not only considered local elites a valuable territorial articulation of national ones (Della Porta D. (2002), *La politica locale*, Il Mulino, Bologna), but underlined the democratic importance of decentralized powers and institutions.
5. Farneti P. (1976), I partiti politici e il sistema di potere, in Castronovo V., a cura di, *L'Italia contemporanea (1945-1975)*, Torino, Einaudi 1976, pp. 61-104 e R. Segatori R., Asfissia di un ceto politico. L'itinerario biografico e politico degli amministratori regionali dell'Umbria (1970-1992), in Bettin G., a cura di, *Classe politica e città*, Padova, Cedam, 1993, pp. 145-178.
6. Cassese S. (2004), Il sistema amministrativo italiano, ovvero l'arte di arrangiarsi, in Cassese S., Franchini C., (eds.), *L'amministrazione pubblica italiana. Un profilo*, Il Mulino, Bologna.
7. Bagnasco A. (1977), *Tre Italie. La problematica territoriale dello sviluppo italiano*, Il Mulino, Bologna; Paci M. (1980), (ed.), *Famiglia e mercato del lavoro in un'economia periferica*, Franco Angeli, Milano.
8. Storper M. (1992), The Limits to Globalization: Technology Districts and International Trade, in *Economic Geography*, n. 1, pp. 60-93.
9. Fabbrini S. (2010), Le élite italiane tra inadeguatezza e trasformazione, in *Stato e Mercato*, n. 2, pp. 343-350; Ciarini A. (2013), *Le politiche sociali nelle regioni italiane. Costanti storiche e trasformazioni recenti*, Il Mulino, Bologna; Ferrera M., Fargion V., Jessoula M. (2012), *Alle radici del welfare all'italiana. Origini e futuro di un modello sociale squilibrato*, Marsilio, Venezia.
10. Riccamboni G. (1976), Regioni, una nuova classe politica?, in *Rivista di sociologia*, n. 1-3, pp. 481-501. Putnam R.D., Leonardi R., Nanetti R. (1985), *La pianta e le radici. Il radicamento dell'istituto regionale nel sistema politico italiano*, Il Mulino Bologna.

11. Nardozzi G. (2004), *Miracolo e declino*, Laterza, Bari-Rom; Trigilia C. (2005), *Sviluppo locale. Un progetto per l'Italia*, Laterza, Roma-Bari.
12. Fargion V. (1997), *Geografia della cittadinanza sociale in Italia*, Il Mulino, Bologna.
13. Very much criticized and discussed, even if at different times, the works of two American authors, Banfield, E.C. (1961), *Una comunità nel mezzogiorno*, Il Mulino, Bologna and Putnam R.D. (1993), *Making Democracy Work: Civic Traditions in Modern Italy,* Princeton, New Jersey, which both highlighted our shortcomings in the associative fabric of civil society in the south of our country, which reverberate on political and electoral tendencies. However, the regions of the north-west and of the Mezzogiorno are characterized by a high level of discontinuity in the voting guidelines and therefore do not have hegemonic or dominant parties.
14. Ferrera M., Fargion V., Jessuola M. (2012).
15. Melis G. (1996), *Storia dell'amministrazione italiana*, Il Mulino, Bologna.
16. The spending review, introduced by the technical government led by Mario Monti, has foreseen heavy cuts in state transfers to local and regional authorities: 2.3 billion in 2012, 5.2 billion in 2013 and 5.5 billion in 2014. The most penalized the regions will be: -1.3 billion in 2012, -2.2 in 2013 and -2.5 in 2014.
17. The cost of the political-bureaucratic apparatus also records important territorial differentiations: the southern regions spend 21.3 per cent of the total regional expenditure (the record is of Sicily: 52.4 per cent), while those of the centre-north 7, 7 per cent. Segatori, *Le debolezze identitarie del regionalismo italiano*, cit. 2010.
18. Eurobarometer (2012), *Public Opinion in the European Union*, n. 76, Bruxelles.
19. In general, italian studies on institutional performance are anchored in Putnam's work (1993). The author focuses on the detection of regional differences in the areas of our country in terms of social capital and institutional performance. The thesis is

that the low quality of the Italian regional institutions of the south compared to those of the center-north is not to be attributed to the economic development gap, as to the smaller amount of social capital (Cartocci R. (2007), *Mappe del tesoro*, Il Mulino, Bologna).

20. Istat (2018), *Poverty in Italy*, Annual Report, Rome.
21. Census (2018), *Health Insurance Report on Public, Private and Intermediary Health*, Rome.
22. National Health Observatory (2017), *XV Annual Report*, Rome.
23. Fondazione Di Vittorio and Tecnè (2016 ), *Report on the Quality of Development in Italy*, Rome.
24. Intesa Sanpaolo for Aspen Institute Italia ( 2015), *The South to Revive: The Experience of the Ex DDR*.
25. Tomasi di Lampedusa, G. (2009), *Il Gattopardo*, Feltrinelli, Milano; Gramsci A. (1996), *Quaderni dal carcere*, Editori Riuniti, Roma.
26. The most pitiless picture of this situation concerns the spending capacity of European structural funds, the main investment tool for the EU's cohesion policy, to foster the economic and employment growth of the Member States and European territorial cooperation. A recent ranking compiled by Corriere della Sera brings together spending data for European funds in the 2014-2020 programming, suggesting that only 880 million of the total 73.6 billion available were used. The total calculation of funds spent in the ERDF (European Regional Development Fund) amounts to zero in Abruzzo, Bolzano, Campania, Lazio, Sicily, Umbria and Puglia: that is, for the most part in regions that would need more other investments.
27. Itinerari previdenziali (2016), *Annual Report on Regionalized Budgets*.
28. Bankitalia (2017), The Economy of Italian Regions. Recent Dynamics and Structural Aspects, *Bulletin* n. 23.
29. OECD (2017), *Science, Technology and Industry Scoreboard*.
30. The reform of Title V of the Constitution has devolved to the Italian regions a series of exclusive or semi-exclusive policy competences, among which health is by far the most relevant.

31. Trigilia C. (1986), *Grandi partiti e piccole imprese*, Il Mulino, Bologna.
32. From Rutelli to Veltroni in Rome, both candidates defeated by Berlusconi to the presidency of the council of ministers, up to Renzi in Florence, who became president of the council, often in recent years, especially the centre-left expressed its leadership of government from men who had held the role of mayor of a large city.
33. Socci M. (2012).
34. Putnam R.D. (1993); Trigilia C. (1986).
35. Socci M. (2012).
36. Sennet R. (2006), *The Culture of the New Capitalism*, Yale University Press, New Haven-London.
37. Lasch C. (1995), *The Revolt of the Elite and the Betrayal of Democracy*, Norton & Company, New York.
38. Carboni C. (2007) (ed.), *Elite e classi dirigenti,* Laterza, Roma Bari.
39. Observing the ranking drawn up by Impresa Lavoro, the region with the highest per capita public spending is Valle d'Aosta, with € 15,731 per year. Followed by Lazio with 13.684 euros, Trentino Alto Adige with 13.278 euros and Friuli Venezia Giulia with 12.975 euros. At the bottom are the largest regions: Lombardy is the last for per-capita public expenditure (8,647 euros), preceded by Veneto (8,734 euros) and Campania (9,082 euros). The ranking changes if the public spending on GDP that each individual region produces is compared. In this case the regions with the highest percentage of public expenditure are Calabria (66.15 per cent), Sardinia (59.9 per cent) and Sicily (56.55 per cent). At the bottom of the list we find the richest regions of the North: Lombardy (where public spending weighs less than 25 per cent), Veneto (29 per cent) and Emilia Romagna (30 per cent) Study Center Impresa Lavoro (2017), *Annual Report*. The per capita debt is on average, for the regions with ordinary statute, of 1,074 euros, for the regions with special status of 1,166 euros. The regions whose inhabitants bear the highest debt are the Val D'Aosta, with 4,632 euros of debt per person, Lazio (3,494 euros) and Piedmont (2,371 euros). Sicily is also above

average (1,581 euros), Campania (1,368 euros) and Molise (1,369 euros). The regions with a lower per capita debt are Lombardy (190 euros), Emilia Romagna (357 euros) and the autonomous province of Trento (365 euros) Italian Court of Auditors (2016), *Report on the Financial Management of the Regions in 2015.*

40. Based on the reworking of the General Accounting Office, a total of 117 MLD can be charged to the regions. Within this ceiling, the region that has spent the most ever has been Sicily with 12.6 MLD, followed by Lombardy with 12.5 MLD, Lazio with 12 MLD, Campania with 10.9 MLD and finally in fifth place Puglia with 7.2. MLD. The regions that spend more than the others to maintain their provinces and municipalities are Lombardy and Campania both on equal merit with 1.62 MLD, Lazio with 1.36 MLD, Sicily with 0.97 MLD and fifth place Piedmont with 0.81 MLD. Instead, by ordering the final expenditure for mission and programmes we would have a different picture of how the resources are absorbed by the government policies adopted in the country. In this case, the first region for absorption of resources would be Lazio with 44 MLD, in second place Lombardy with 37 MLD, third and fourth place, almost equal, Sicily and Campania with 22 MLD, and finally Piedmont with 16 MLD. (*Regionalized State Budget 2014*).

41. The missions represent the strategic objectives pursued with public spending. They are, therefore, a political-institutional representation of the budget, aimed at making the large aggregates of expenditure more transparent and communicating the main lines of administrative action of the individual administrations. Each mission is usually divided into several programmes, but there are missions that consist of a single programme. The programmes represent homogeneous aggregates of activities carried out within each individual ministry, to pursue well-defined objectives within the institutional scope. They are predominantly the responsibility of a single ministry, even if there are no programmes shared between several administrations.

# Conclusion

The snapshot we have taken of Italy paints a picture of a plural country composed of local areas, communities and development systems which differ in terms of social culture, institutional performance and political particularism (chaotic polycentrism). While this characteristic can be seen in the context of the long course of history, at the same time it is the product of the political circumstances and their influence on development. The diversity of "Italys" speaks not only of structures and continuity but also of events and changes. From this perspective, this essay has focused on three strategic aspects which may provide guidance for the future.

The first aspect identifies a "narrow pathway" in the Italian model of local development, a crossroads in the globalization of markets which imposes an either/or choice: decline or change? The Italy of the industrial districts constitutes an innovative experience of growth in the country's manufacturing structure and entrepreneurial density. At the same time, this development was activated upon a centuries-old layering of economic, cultural, social, institutional and technological backwardness. Local development took advantage of historic opportunities arising in a regime of narrow-mindedness, and the result was an industrial continuation of the rural organization of factors of production. This brought together—without apparent contradiction—a diverse miscellany of pre-modern and modern factors. Informal economies were accompanied and sustained by state policies to incentivize redistribution (for small businesses and small farms); age-old, static working cultures rapidly gave way to the goal of widespread inclination to risk, enhancing the capacity of the middle classes and urban artisans to develop economically (in self-employment and small manufacturing enterprises); local employment markets mobilized resources and workers using pre-industrial regulatory factors based on loyalty, obedience and belonging; these in turn were mediated by family-based structures and networks of loyalty to friends, family and neighbourhood. What for many years appeared to be a happy, complementary and painless transition between tradition and innovation is today seen in a different, more critical light. The structural backwardness does not appear to be remedied by the albeit important steps taken by firms, as newcomers to development. Even though they operate in different socio-cultural contexts and with critical masses that make them incomparable with Italy, the world's economic giants—the new players in world development, emerged in the past three decades—are affected by the virtues and limitations of late-developing economies. The faults caused by the backwardness of Italian society and economy are a litmus test for phenomena with a wider impact on world economic development. A lack of transparency in the competitive mindset, widespread political marketeering, corruption, poor institutional coordination of public money, failures in the education and training of human resources and little inclination towards a culture of innovation are aspects afflicting the country and, in various ways, also impacting the local development of the regions and the ways in which the economic crisis played out within them. An examination of these dynamics and their effects on society is a kind of indirect estimation of the shape world development might take in the decades to come, likely to be characterized by an increasingly central role of economies built on the basis of underdevelopment.

The recent cycle of Italian industrial production was characterized by the occurrence of two major recessions which, between April 2008 and November 2013, led to a fall of 24 per cent in production, a decrease which took the rate below the figures for the early 1990s. In Italy this drop in output had greater repercussions than in many of its EU partner states: the latter saw the greatest fall in production in 2012, while 2013 brought relative stabilization and, in some cases, modest recovery. Italy, however, technically came out of recession only in 2015, but with a very modest increase in GDP, not enough to overturn the ongoing contraction in domestic demand.[1]

Regarding local and regional systems, the crisis highlighted a difference in the speed of response between regions that reacted well to the crisis and others which struggled far more. Local governance in general seemed weak, with very few instances of excellence (e.g. Emilia Romagna), where the political class and local administration were instrumental in activating social innovation (with local welfare policies) and supporting technological development (e.g. the regional network of digital innovation for business and manufacturing). If we focus attention on the Adriatic corridor of development and the so-called Third Italy, regions such as Veneto and Emilia Romagna—and Tuscany, with much more difficulty—succeeded in remaining in line with the continental platform of the European economy. Conversely, production models such as those in the Marche and Umbria seem to stagnate in their localism, moving further away from the crucial European economy. The question which places the risk of decline against the opportunity for a change in direction is played out in terms of social and business culture and technology. Inflated localism and sidelining in the frontiers of innovation are the knots to be unravelled in order to prevent delays and peripherality in development. The Italian production system and its employment market appear to be trapped in a situation of sub-optimal equilibrium which is difficult to escape, despite the availability of potentially more efficient alternatives. In the case of businesses, this locked-in effect is predominantly technological. Firms are suffering from investment in technologies proven to be inferior to other available alternatives and entailing high fixed costs, as well as from negative externalities caused by connected groups of companies which use the same (obsolete or less efficient) technology. The high costs of negotiation hinders the movement towards another standard which is more efficient and effective.

Nevertheless, the time for thinking of local development through the lens of "localism" has run out. The immaterial economy, globalization and the farsighted and interconnected organisation of successful companies require a transformation in both business culture and governance. Besides demonstrating the power that contingent events exert over long-term continuity, the crisis underlined that the district-based economy is not a homogeneous unit differentiated merely by the configuration of production processes. On the contrary, it constitutes a local milieu in which the factors of the culture of institutional innovation and technological research make all the difference. The social and local differentiation in the ability of Italian local systems to respond proactively to the crisis of the past decade is symptomatic of the lack of structural homogeneity between regions and consequently their varying capacity to perform in terms of economics and policy-making. The culture of innovation remains anchored to a model of "innovation without research" which worked in the past in the traditional sectors of the economy, but which is no longer sustainable. The contribution of science and technology to the valorization of goods, products and processes and the creation of professional communities is drawing new maps of international competitiveness, and Italy seems to be peripheral to this. The whole situation is aggravated by the enduring division of the Italian economy between areas that are highly advanced and integrated in the continental European platform, and pockets of underdevelopment in many southern regions. While the numerous "pocket-sized multinationals" of the Made in Italy movement are the competitive flagship of the Italian economy in the wider world, the equally numerous scattered production chains of semi-marginal small traditional firms are the other face of an entrenched economic backwardness. Add to this the persisting inefficiencies in public finance and the many large private-sector groups that operate within it. This all looks like the consequences of a system based on an excess of political capitalism, often bordering on the dynamics of corruption or even complicity with criminal activity.

The second, more theoretical aspect concerns the possibility of rebuilding the institutional foundations of local development by freeing it from a rigid course of path dependence. From this viewpoint, the furrow of history, like a railway line, guides the course taken by institutions in the *longue durée*, which always remains the same.[2] Conversely, our examination seeks to reevaluate the role of collective social practices, innovative economic and entrepreneurial phenomena and business decisions based on the circumstances of economic development and institutional performance. The economy and the market are rooted in society but not in the "theological" terms of structures that withstand time and reproduce systematically, forever conditioning the social and institutional life of the communities in which they operate. Individuals, communities and institutions are the fruit of human practices which recursively build structures (Durand), rather than simply being influenced by them (Levi-Strauss).[3] This means that change and innovation are as much a part of history as the repetition of phenomena that can withstand and endure over time (e.g. institutions). For structures, time seems to stand still, yet when the historian or sociologist observes the structures that succeed each other in the course of history, they describe the trajectory of irreversible transformation that marks the decline of one structure and the dawn of another which replaces it.[4] History is a series of institutionalisations and their reverse; in other words a repetition of the change that conditions the social, economic, cultural and existential geography of every age and its inhabitants. Nothing is immune to transformation over time and nothing in the formation of institutions is valid as incontrovertible truth.

For example, the existence of strong links and substantial stocks of social capital is not always favourable to development. Cultural values and social customs are crucial to allow such networks to become facilitators and activators of the economy. The behaviour and actions of members of a network and the institutional rules of the context within which they operate take on a critical role both in the performance of institutions (the production and distribution of wealth)[5] and in the methods used to produce public policy based on governance.[6] The latter can be considered a kind of exogenous shock, able to inoculate the local context with new organizational capabilities and cognitive frames which can destabilise the path dependencies and their sub-optimal restrictions.[7] The establishment of new governance-based models of policy-making has included non-state bodies in decision-making processes, increasing the opportunities for cooperation between public and private sectors in the interests of competitiveness. However, this does not prevent the risk of inappropriate mixing between the two, which casts a certain amount of scepticism on the true democratic nature of local governance, particularly due to the danger of a potential decline into particularism and profiteering.[8]

Finally, the third aspect concerns the role of politics in the activation, sustaining and consolidation of the economy, as well as the risk of failure in its institutions.

The path-dependency model relegates politics to a narrow space, neutralizing its impact on the outcomes of economic development. Politics and those who run it do not merely have the unwelcome possibility of deserting and thus destroying the pool of deep-rooted social capital accumulated over time. On the contrary, they can play an innovative, situational and structural role in terms of the quality and effectiveness of governance. All the more reason why Italian regions that have implemented some of the most effective local welfare systems in the world (Emilia Romagna) are followed by others whose retardation compared to the most successful domestic economies (the north-western regions) has not changed in the past 157 years of Italian unity.

For good or for evil, politics as a dimension of power and politicians as institutional actors (or ruling classes) have fundamental merits and faults for the outcomes—including in the short term—of the local communities they govern. Only in this way can we correctly consider Italy in the plural.

## REFERENCES

1. ISTAT (2014), *Rapporto sulla competitività dei settori produttivi*, Roma.
2. Putnam R.D. (1993), *Making Democracy Work: Civic Traditions in Modern Italy,* Princeton University Press.
3. Durand G. (1963), *Les structures anthropologiques de l'immaginaire*, Presses Universitaires de France.; Lévi-Strauss C. (1958), *Anthropologiestructurale*, Plon, Paris.
4. Pomian K. (2006), *Histoire des structures*, en Le Goff J. (ed.) (2006), *La Nouvelle Histoire*, Complexe, Paris.
5. Smith-Doerr Laurel and Walter Powell, 2005. Networks and Economic Life, pp. 379–402 in *The Handbook of Economic Sociology*, Second Edition, (ed.) Neil Smelser and Richard Swedberg, Princeton University Press, Princeton, NJ.

6. Lynn Laurence E., Jr., Ingraham P.W. (2004), Governance and Public Management: A Symposium, *Journal of Policy Analysis and Management* 23(1): 3–96; Macedo S. (1999), *Deliberative Politics: Essays on Democracy and Disagreement*. Oxford University Press, New York; March J.G., Olsen J.P. (1995), *Democratic Governance*, Free Press, New York.
7. Virili F., Sorrentino M. (2009), Value Generation in E-government from Service-Based IT Integration, *Transforming Government: People, Process and Policy*, 3:3 (2009), pp. 227-247.
8. Crouch C. (2004), *Post Democracy*, Polity Press.